In 2011 Flic (then girlfriend, now wife) and I bought an old food van and The Jabberwocky was born. We started out with the hope of spending a little more time together and seeing some new local events. By Easter 2013 I had quit my job as a chef and soon we were both working for ourselves; making a living out of selling toasties. After nearly a decade of making toasted sandwiches I think we can safely call ourselves experts.

We chose to cook and serve toasties primarily because of my genuine obsession with them. They are also the ultimate street foood: they are portable, need no cutlery nor crockery to enjoy, are eaten one-handed (leaving the other hand to do whatever it needs to) and can contain anything you want. This means you are able to cater for every taste and dietary requirement out there. This is a collection of 50 of our favourite fillings and combinations. These are all tried and tested recipes that have been sold to the Great British public at least once.

During 2015 Flic wrote a book about starting a street food business called "Street Food Soliloquy". While she was working on it I started writing a toastie cook book. It was mostly to keep myself out of her way. I never thought I would get round to finishing or publishing it. However, that was before 2020 happened. This book became my lock down project and now after 5 years (and a pandemic) I am finally ready for you to read it.

First Printed 2020

Published by B Luxmoore

ISBN 9798552285709

www.thejabberwocky.co.uk

This is a rare first edition

For Flic
You're a towel

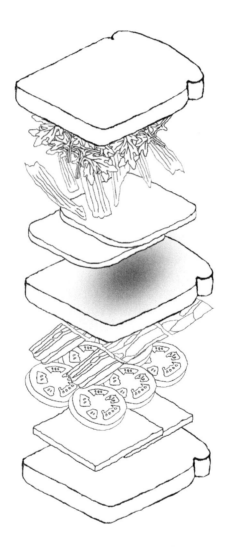

Toastie Construction Manual
By
Barny Luxmoore

Contents

B4:Sauce Components   111

B5: Dessert Components   120

Introduction

Welcome to the Toastie Construction Manual. This book has been organised into an instruction book as glossy photos of melted cheese are lovely to look at, but are not much help when making toasties.

The manual is organised in 3 sections. Section A are the actual toastie recipes, Section B is details on how to make any of the compound components and section C is all the other information that you might need.

All the toasties in Section A have a similar layout to below. The most important part is the exploded diagram of each sandwich (also the most useful when building). The ingredient quantities are based on the toasties we make for sale and on the giant bread that we use for commercial purposes. You may find that the amounts need to be tweaked to suit your personal tastes and the bread you are using.

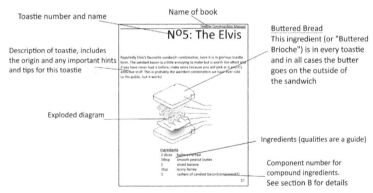

Now is the point in all recipe books where the author insists on rambling about all sorts of subjects rather than getting on with the recipes. Now that I am writing the recipe book I have realised there are many important topics to discuss before making toasties. However, I am aware that most readers don't care, so all these thoughts on butter, cheese, bread, toastie makers and why sliced is better than grated cheese, can be found at in Section C (if you wish to read them). If you have never made a toastie before, Section C is essential reading before you start making sandwiches.

Section A: Toastie Construction Instructions

A1 Red Meat

Nº1: Ham and Cheese

This is the only place to start a book about toasties. It is the classic combination and our best seller by a country mile. This sandwich (in some form) has been invented in most countries in the world and they will all tell you that their version is the best. Whichever version you make; the best ham and cheese toasties are made from ham that you have cooked yourself. However, it seems unlikely that you will ever want to make the 100 toasties that make this a worthwhile activity. Therefore, I recommend buying pre-sliced ham. But for the love of cheese, don't get cheap re-formed slices from the supermarket. It is worth spending a little more. When you eat your creation you will not be disappointed. I prefer a single thicker slice of ham, but only do this if it is good quality and you will be able to bite through it easily.

Ingredients

40g	sliced ham
75g	cheddar
2 slices	buttered bread

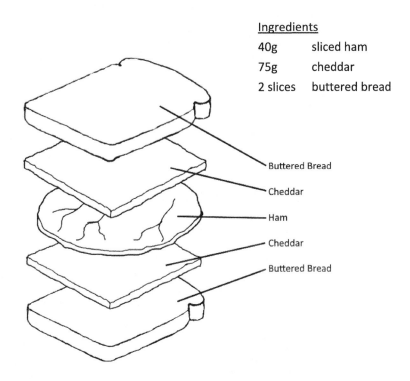

Buttered Bread
Cheddar
Ham
Cheddar
Buttered Bread

N^o2: Bacon, Brie and Cranberry

Another classic combination. This is not ground breaking, but it is delicious. If you are dubious about the cranberry, but have never tried this combo, then give it a go and it will surprise you in a good way. The trick with this toastie is smoked, streaky bacon, cooked until it is good and crispy before being used in the toastie.

Ingredients

2slices	buttered bread
75g	brie
1tsp	cranberry sauce
3	smoked streaky bacon rashers (chopped in 3)

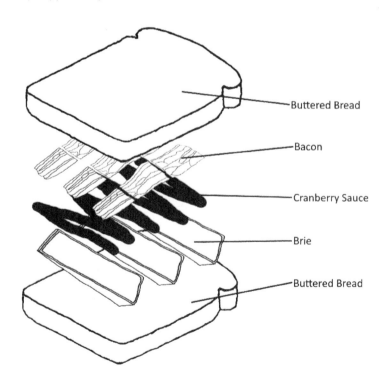

Buttered Bread

Bacon

Cranberry Sauce

Brie

Buttered Bread

Nº3:The Cuban

This is our version of a classic sandwich, popular in the USA, and unsurprisingly originally from Cuba. It is effectively a pimped up ham and cheese. A lot of people will say they don't like mustard (or gherkin), but give it a go and then judge. Flic hates mustard and admits this is better with it than without. However, you don't need much! The gherkins are best if diced up so that you don't bite half way into one and pull it out.

Ingredients

2 slices	buttered bread
40g	cheddar
40g	Monterey Jack
½	pickled gherkin (diced)
¼ tsp	English mustard
40g	pulled pork
	(component 2)

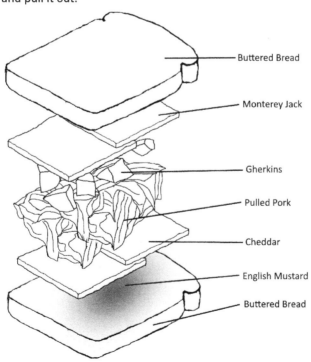

Buttered Bread

Monterey Jack

Gherkins

Pulled Pork

Cheddar

English Mustard

Buttered Bread

Nº4: Slow Roast Pork and Sage Derby

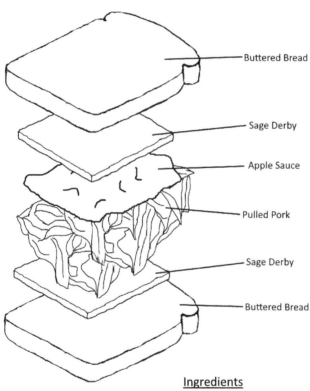

Buttered Bread

Sage Derby

Apple Sauce

Pulled Pork

Sage Derby

Buttered Bread

This toastie was made to celebrate the lovely Sage Derby cheese made by our cheese supplier, Fowler's. This can be bought in various shops and markets in the Midlands. If you can't get hold of it, Cheddar and a bit of fresh sage make a decent alternative.

Ingredients

2 slices	buttered bread
1tbsp	apple sauce
60g	Fowler's sage derby
75g	pulled pork
	(component 2)

Nº5: The Elvis

Reputedly Elvis's favourite sandwich combination, here it is in glorious toastie form. The candied bacon is a little annoying to make but is worth the effort and if you have never had it before; make extra because you will pick at it and it's addictive stuff. This is probably the weirdest combination we have ever sold to the public, but it works!

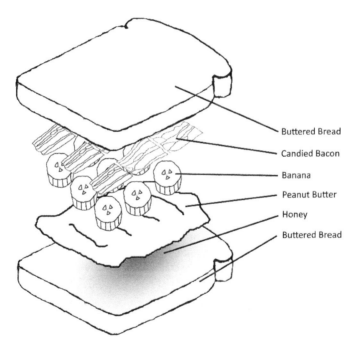

Buttered Bread

Candied Bacon

Banana

Peanut Butter

Honey

Buttered Bread

Ingredients

2 slices	buttered bread
1tbsp	smooth peanut butter
1	banana 15mm slices
1tsp	runny honey
3 rashers	candied bacon (component 3)

Nº6: The Club

Once again, our take on a classic sandwich. As this has a middle layer of bread and it is going to be a toastie the 3rd slice needs to be toasted before use. This recipe is not suitable for traditional toastie machines as it is too thick so you will not be able to close the lid properly.

Ingredients

2 slices	buttered bread
1 slice	toast
40g	cheddar
40g	mozzarella
2rasher	smoked bacon (chopped)
20g	rocket
1	fresh tomato (sliced)
1tbsp	mayo
50g	roast chicken (component 4)

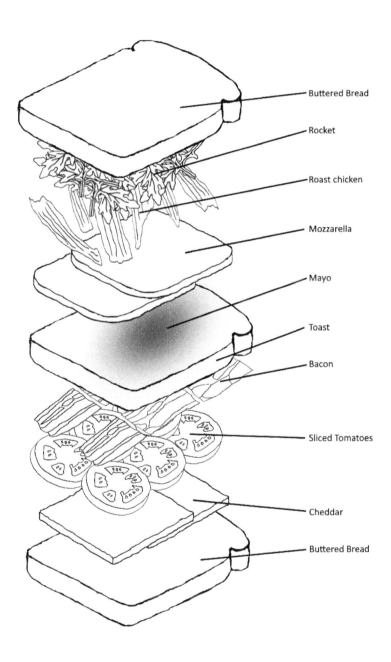

Buttered Bread

Rocket

Roast chicken

Mozzarella

Mayo

Toast

Bacon

Sliced Tomatoes

Cheddar

Buttered Bread

Nº7: Beef and Stilton

This very British toastie demonstrates the best way to get stilton into a grilled sandwich. Stilton does not melt well (it tends to go greasy and lumpy) and has an over powering taste. However, if you love blue cheese this is a way of making a spread that is perfect for toasties. It's also excellent on a cheese scone.

The toastie is obviously better with homemade piccalilli, but I don't think it is worth the hassle when you can go to any farmers market and buy a jar. Or if you can't make it to a market the Haywards version (available from every supermarket) is perfect for this recipe.

When making shake a little salt over the beef once it's in the sandwich, it makes all the difference.

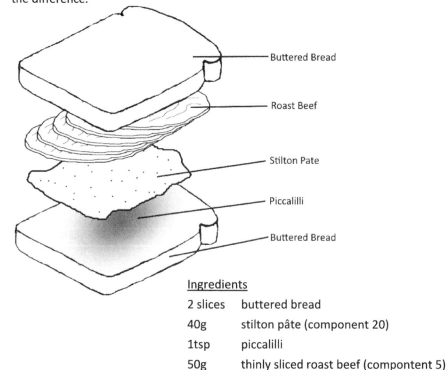

Buttered Bread

Roast Beef

Stilton Pate

Piccalilli

Buttered Bread

Ingredients

2 slices	buttered bread
40g	stilton pâte (component 20)
1tsp	piccalilli
50g	thinly sliced roast beef (compontent 5)

Nº8: Corned beef

Sounds weird, but honestly it's lovely. Some credit should also go to my university friend Tony, who gave me the origianl idea while living together in Leeds.

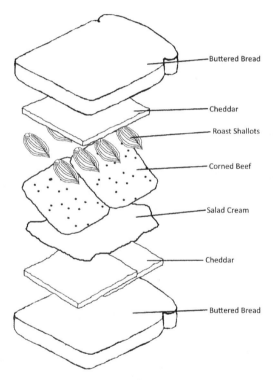

- Buttered Bread
- Cheddar
- Roast Shallots
- Corned Beef
- Salad Cream
- Cheddar
- Buttered Bread

Ingredients

2slices	buttered bread
50g	corned beef – 5mm slices
1tsp	salad cream
60g	cheddar
1	roasted shallot (component 21)

Nº9: Venison and Cumberland Sauce

This toastie uses the best value (cheapest) part of the animal, but that does mean that you have to cook the meat for a while to get the most out of it. I think this is the best way to eat venison. As a very lean game meat, a toastie is a great way of getting a little more fat into the mix without drowning it in butter.

Ingredients

2slices	buttered bread
60g	braised venison (component 6)
60g	double gloucester
50g	mushroom mix (component 30)
1tbsp	Cumberland sauce (component 35)

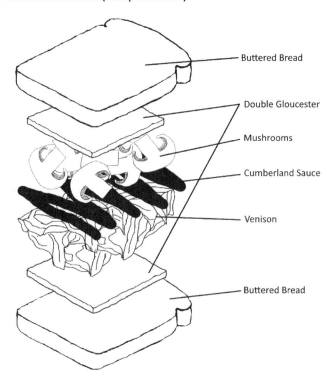

Buttered Bread

Double Gloucester

Mushrooms

Cumberland Sauce

Venison

Buttered Bread

Nº10: The Reuben

There is no definitive answer as to what goes into this classic New York sandwich. We tried a lot of combinations and this was by far our favourite, based on the products you can get this side of the pond. This one is great on Rye bread if you can get a good one.

The following recipe is based on super market standard pastrami. If you can get a better one; do it as this will make the toastie. Note that Russian dressing; is neither a dressing nor Russian, in fact it is American. It's just thousand island sauce with extra mustard A.K.A. Big Mac sauce.

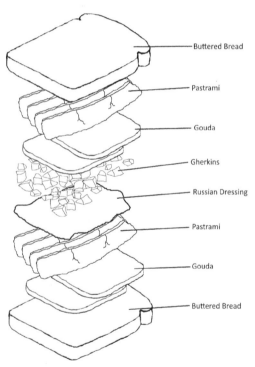

Buttered Bread

Pastrami

Gouda

Gherkins

Russian Dressing

Pastrami

Gouda

Buttered Bread

Ingredients

2 slices	buttered bread
75g	gouda
1dsp	gherkins (diced)
8 slices	pastrami – thinly sliced
1tsp	Russian dressing (component 36)

Nº11: The Breakfast Toastie

One of the few toasties that doesn't require cheese, although it is still good on this one, so feel free to slip a little inside. The ingredients are easier to deal with cold, so I recommend making them up the night before and then having them as a hangover-busting breakfast the next day. Use the meat to form a barrier between bread and bean juice.

Ingredients

2 slices	buttered bread
2	cooked sausages, chilled and sliced lengthways
2	smoked bacon cooked and cut into 3 pieces
1dsp	Heinz beans

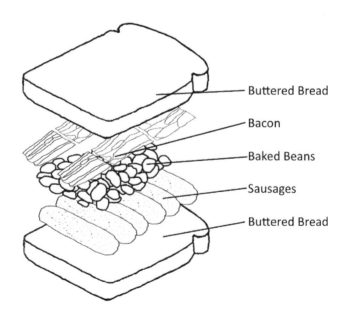

- Buttered Bread
- Bacon
- Baked Beans
- Sausages
- Buttered Bread

№12: Chorizo and Jalapeños

Simple and delicious. The recipe that follows is based on marinated jalapeños (which can be found in most supermarkets). If you can't get hold of any, the same recipe also works with sliced fresh green chillies.

Ingredients

2slices	buttered bread
60g	mozzarella
6slices	chorizo (thin slices)
6 slices	jalapeños
½tsp	garlic puree

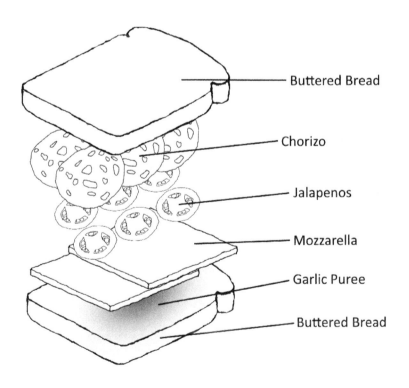

Buttered Bread

Chorizo

Jalapenos

Mozzarella

Garlic Puree

Buttered Bread

Nº13: The Meaty Package

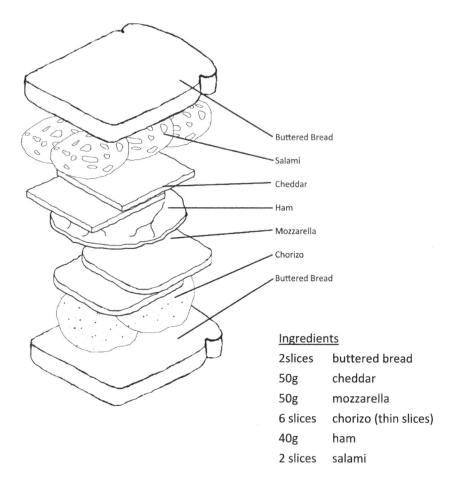

Buttered Bread
Salami
Cheddar
Ham
Mozzarella
Chorizo
Buttered Bread

Ingredients

2 slices	buttered bread
50g	cheddar
50g	mozzarella
6 slices	chorizo (thin slices)
40g	ham
2 slices	salami

A regular customer once told us (as a joke) that we should have a toastie called Barny's Meaty Package. We thought it was a great name so we used it, it also demonstrates how much better something sells with a good name. This used be the "meat feast", but this sells better!

Nº14:Lamb and Feta

For this toastie to work the creamed feta is essential. "Raw feta" can be used, but it will to overpower everything else in the toastie and standard feta doesn't melt well. Plus the creamed feta helps keep all the other ingredients inside the sandwich.

This toastie really benefits from being made with brown bread.

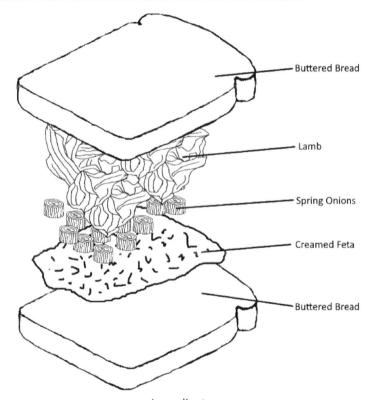

Buttered Bread

Lamb

Spring Onions

Creamed Feta

Buttered Bread

Ingredients

2slices	buttered bread
70g	braised lamb (component 7)
2tbsp	creamed feta (component 19)
1	spring onion (chopped)

Nº15: The Kofta Toastie

These are our standard koftas and make a lovely meal with some salad and pitta bread. But in a toastie they are even better. Don't be afraid to put in lots of Manchego it's a mild cheese, but works brilliantly in this combination.

<u>Ingredients</u>

2 slices	buttered bread
4	lamb kofta (component 8)
50g	manchego
25g	roast peppers (component 22)
1tbsp	raita - mint yogurt (component 37)

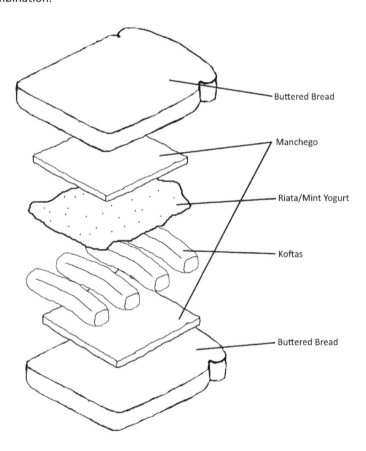

Buttered Bread

Manchego

Riata/Mint Yogurt

Koftas

Buttered Bread

Nº16: Scotch Egg Toastie

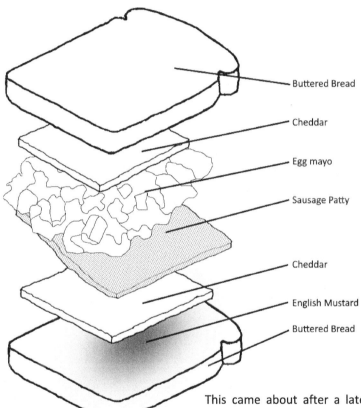

- Buttered Bread
- Cheddar
- Egg mayo
- Sausage Patty
- Cheddar
- English Mustard
- Buttered Bread

Ingredients

2slices	buttered bread
1tbsp	egg mayo (component 34)
1	sausage patty (cooked)
75g	cheddar
1tsp	English mustard

This came about after a late night snack, that shouldn't have been nice. The original had a scotch egg sliced up and thrown in a toastie with some cheese. From there we have refined it. This sandwich was an gold award winner in the toasted sandwich category at The Cafélife Awards in 2015. The sausage patty is the contents of a sausage removed from its skin and grilled (alternatively use a Lorne sausage).

Nº17: Oktoberfest

Originally created for a production at a small theatre. The play (Twilight of the Freaking Gods) was based on an opera by Wagner. They asked us to create a toastie for the event. So we made the most German sandwich we could. We liked the toastie so much that it comes back every year in autumn. It is possible to make your own sauerkraut, but in the words of my German sister-in-law "Why would you bother? When you can buy it from the supermarket".

I recommend Lidl or Aldi for the ingredients (to this one) as then you get proper German brands.

The bratwurst needs to be precooked and chilled so it can be easily sliced.

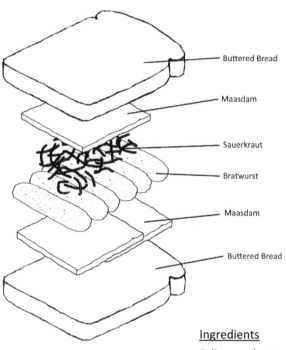

Buttered Bread

Maasdam

Sauerkraut

Bratwurst

Maasdam

Buttered Bread

Ingredients

2slices	buttered bread
60g	maasdam Cheese
1	bratwurst – sliced long ways
25g	sauerkraut

Nº18: Water Buffalo

This was invented after meeting another trader who raise and sell their own water buffalo. When you find out there is a buffalo farm less than 10 miles from your house. You have to invent a toastie to show case it properly. If you can't get water buffalo the pulled beef is a good alternative.

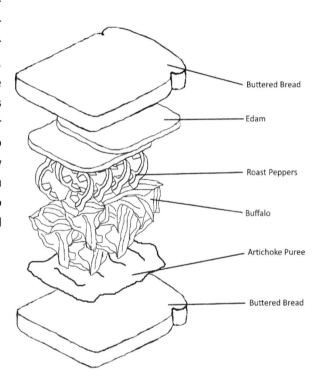

Buttered Bread

Edam

Roast Peppers

Buffalo

Artichoke Puree

Buttered Bread

Ingredients

2 slices	buttered bread
40g	braised buffalo (component 12)
20g	roasted peppers (component 22)
1tbsp	artichoke and garlic puree (component 29)
50g	edam

A2 Fish and Seafood

Nº19: Tuna Melt

Another classic given the Jabberwocky treatment. So good that it won "Highly Commended" in 2017 at the British Sandwich Awards. It is a great toastie, but beware of storing it for more than a couple of hours. The moisture from the tuna can ruin your bread. Keep this in mind when you are putting the toastie together and try to spread out the cheese slice so you cover as much bread as possible. To help with this we chop each slice of cheese up into 3 and spread it out a little.

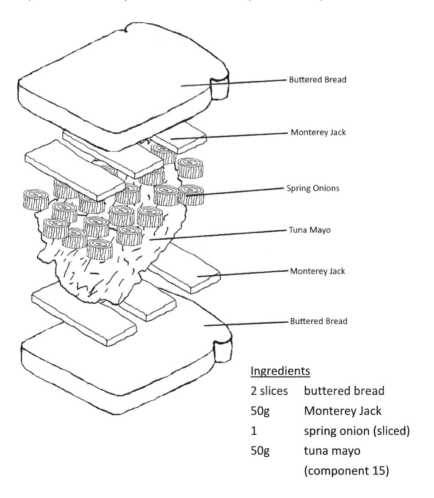

Buttered Bread

Monterey Jack

Spring Onions

Tuna Mayo

Monterey Jack

Buttered Bread

Ingredients

2 slices	buttered bread
50g	Monterey Jack
1	spring onion (sliced)
50g	tuna mayo
	(component 15)

Nº20: Prawn and Chorizo Cocktail

The normal contents of a prawn cocktail plus cheese and chorizo in a toastie. Most people are dubious about the chorizo, but we think it makes this toastie come alive.

This melt is meant to be made with small prawns, not king prawns. You can use the big ones but it doesn't quite taste right. Make sure that your ingredients are as dry as possible before using.

Ingredients

2 slices	buttered bread
6 slices	chorizo – thin slices
30g	north atlantic prawns
20g	watercress
50g	mozzarella
1dsp	marie-rose (component 38)

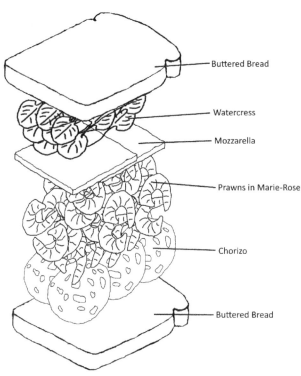

Buttered Bread

Watercress

Mozzarella

Prawns in Marie-Rose

Chorizo

Buttered Bread

Nº21: Smoked Salmon

This toastie was originally created to show off the amazing smoked salmon that is made by a friend of ours at "The Woodland Kitchen", just down the road. As you probably can't get that stuff I would recommend getting any good quality hot-smoked salmon instead. Cold smoked also works if you prefer. If you can't get baby leaf spinach, you can use any other spinach; you just have to wilt it first.

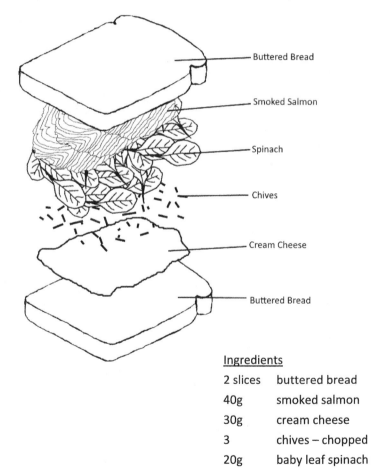

Buttered Bread

Smoked Salmon

Spinach

Chives

Cream Cheese

Buttered Bread

Ingredients

2 slices	buttered bread
40g	smoked salmon
30g	cream cheese
3	chives – chopped
20g	baby leaf spinach

Nº22: Dressed Crab with Mascarpone

Not much to say about this toastie. It is delicous, but relies on good quality crab meat for the main flavour. Watch out as the fillings are moist so needs to be made and cooked soon after... not one for storing!

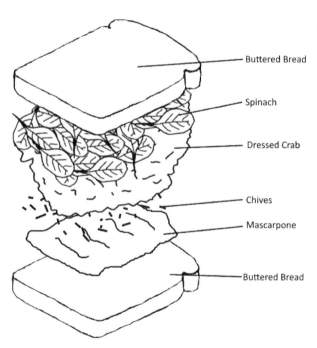

Buttered Bread

Spinach

Dressed Crab

Chives

Mascarpone

Buttered Bread

Ingredients

2 slices	buttered bread
30g	dressed crab
2dsp	mascarpone
25g	washed baby leaf spinach
1tsp	chopped fresh chives

Nº23: Crayfish

This sounds really fancy and it has some complex flavours, but it is easy to make. To get a better mixing of flavours it helps to pre-mix the hummus and the pesto. Crayfish tails can be a bit tricky to get hold of, but they are worth the effort.

Ingredients

2 slices	buttered bread
40g	crayfish tails
25g	hummus
1tsp	pesto
2	sun-dried tomatoes – roughly chopped
50g	mozzarella

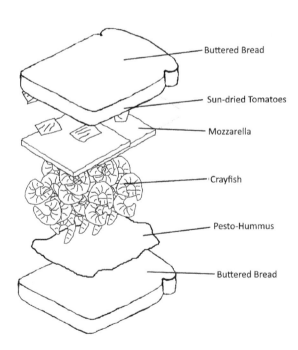

- Buttered Bread
- Sun-dried Tomatoes
- Mozzarella
- Crayfish
- Pesto-Hummus
- Buttered Bread

Nº24: Scallops & Black Pudding

This toastie combines 2 classic restaurant combinations for scallops; black pudding and cauliflower. It is great way of using cheaper, smaller queen scallops rather than the larger kings.

Ingredients

2 slices	buttered bread
6	queen scallops (component 18)
50g	cheese sauce (component 41)
6 slices	cauliflower (component 28)
2	large black pudding slices (as thin as possible)
25g	mozzarella

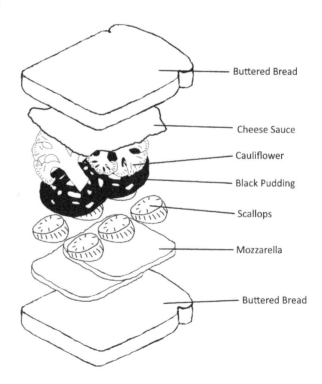

Buttered Bread

Cheese Sauce

Cauliflower

Black Pudding

Scallops

Mozzarella

Buttered Bread

Nº25:Lobster Thermidor

The most indulgent and expensive toastie we have ever made! We have taken the classic lobster Thermidor and crossed it with an American-style lobster roll to create a really special sandwich.

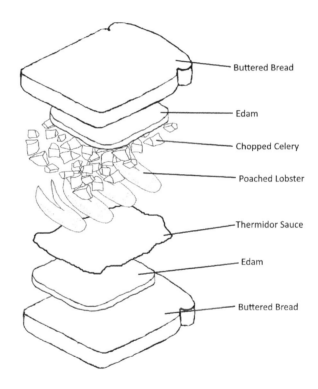

- Buttered Bread
- Edam
- Chopped Celery
- Poached Lobster
- Thermidor Sauce
- Edam
- Buttered Bread

Ingredients

2 slices	buttered bread
1tsp	grated parmesan
50g	edam
1tbsp	thermidor sauce (Component 40)
50g	poached lobster (Component 17)
2tsp	celery (finely diced)

A3 Poultry and Game Birds

Nº26: Chicken Parmesan

Middlesbrough is famous for only one food: the "Parmo". Here is our homage to the local delicacy of my childhood.

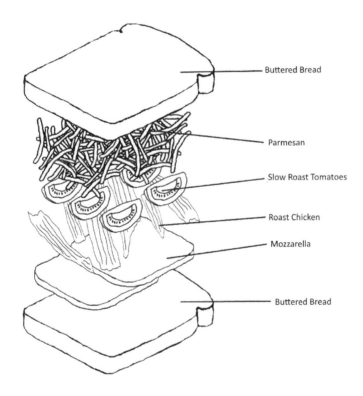

Buttered Bread

Parmesan

Slow Roast Tomatoes

Roast Chicken

Mozzarella

Buttered Bread

Ingredients

2 slices	buttered bread
60g	roast chicken (component 4)
5 pieces	slow roast tomatoes (component 24)
50g	mozzarella
1tbsp	parmesan (grated)

Nº27: Barbeque Chicken

Our starting point for this toastie was the BBQ sauce that I first made to go on some pulled pork baps, but we liked the sauce so much, we decided to make a toastie to show it off. Since then it has become a firm favourite of ours and our customers.

The BBQ sauce might sound like a lot of work, but it is worth the effort as is so much nicer than shop bought.

Ingredients

2 slices	buttered bread
2tbsp	BBQ sauce (component 42)
15g	streaky bacon (cooked & chopped)
20g	sweet corn
60g	roast chicken (component 4)
40g	gruyere (or cheddar)
50g	mozzarella

To make this toastie less messy and taste a whole lot better; pre-mix the sauce, bacon, sweet corn and chicken before using it in the sandwich (BBQ chicken mix in the diagram).

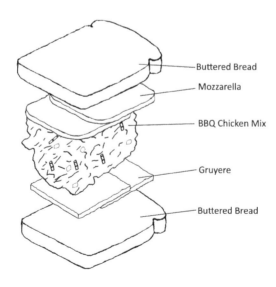

Buttered Bread
Mozzarella
BBQ Chicken Mix
Gruyere
Buttered Bread

Nº28: Xmas Toastie-
Turkey & Camembert

Classic combination of turkey, camembert and cranberry. Simple, delicious and tastes like Xmas.

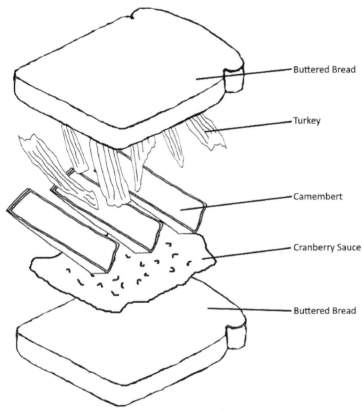

Buttered Bread

Turkey

Camembert

Cranberry Sauce

Buttered Bread

Ingredients

2 slices	buttered bread
70g	roast turkey (component 9)
80g	camembert
1tbsp	cranberry sauce

NO29: Smoked Pigeon

It is unlikely that you will find somewhere selling smoked pigeon breasts so if you want to try this, you are going to have to get smoking! It is definitely much better with smoked pigeon than any other kind.

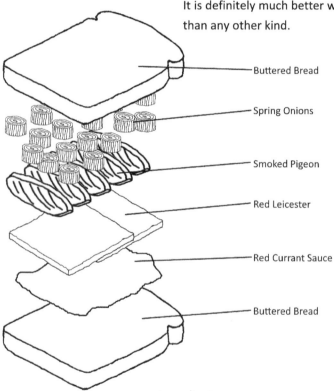

Buttered Bread

Spring Onions

Smoked Pigeon

Red Leicester

Red Currant Sauce

Buttered Bread

Ingredients

2slices	buttered bread
1	smoked pigeon breast (component 10)
50g	red Leicester
1	spring onion (roughly chopped)
2tsp	redcurrant Jelly

Nº30: Pheasant and Black Pudding

One of our all-time favourite toasties. Even if you don't like black pudding (or spring onion) give it a go as it might just change your mind. This combination cannot be topped.

Ingredients

2 slices	buttered bread
40g	roast pheasant (component 11)
6 slices	black pudding (thin slices)
1	spring onion (chopped)
50g	cheddar

Buttered Bread

Spring Onions

Pheasant

Black Pudding

Cheddar

Buttered Bread

A4 Vegetarian

Nº31: The Italian Summer

Our most popular veggie toastie. The secret is to use the mozzarella as a barrier to stop the liquid from the peppers making the bread soggy and gross. Make sure to use dry mozzarella rather than the wet balls for the same reason. If you can't be bothered to roast peppers, you can buy them ready to use from most supermarkets.

Ingredients

2 slices	buttered bread
70g	mozzarella
1	roast pepper (component 22)
1tsp	pesto

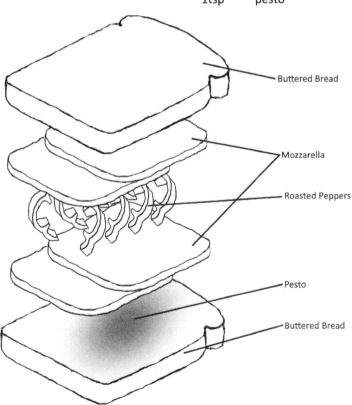

Buttered Bread

Mozzarella

Roasted Peppers

Pesto

Buttered Bread

N^o32: 4 Cheese Supreme

This is the scientifically chosen best combination of 4 cheeses that we could find. In the process of development we tried 29 combinations of various cheeses. The mix we ended up with was not as exotic as had hoped when we started out, but this was definitely the best combo we found. One day we might re-visit it now we know a little more, but that is for the next cook book.

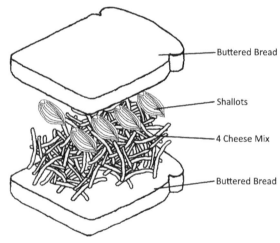

Buttered Bread

Shallots

4 Cheese Mix

Buttered Bread

Ingredients

2 slices	buttered bread
40g	emmental
40g	cheddar
40g	mozzarella (dry block)
10g	parmesan
1	roast shallot (component 21)

This one of the rare times that grated cheese is a must. The only way to get the best out of the cheese mix is to grate it and then toss in a bowl, so that the cheeses are properly mixed together.

This recipe can be made by substituting caramelised onions (component 33) for the shallots. I prefer this with onions, but they are a devisive ingredient and a lot of people prefer neither.

Nº33: Feta and Olives

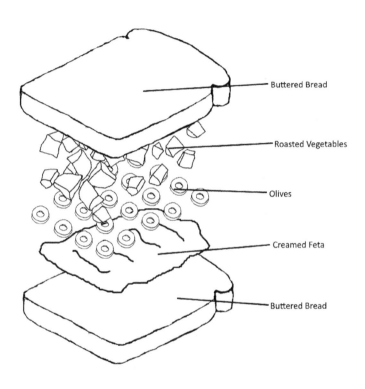

- Buttered Bread
- Roasted Vegetables
- Olives
- Creamed Feta
- Buttered Bread

Ingredients

2 slices	buttered bread
50g	creamed feta (component 19)
4	black and green olives (sliced)
25g	roasted med veg (component 23)

If you hate olives you can leave them out, personally I think marinated garlic cloves also work here.

Nº34: Brie, Tomato & Basil

The first vegetarian toastie we ever sold to the public and still my favoruite of our meat free options.

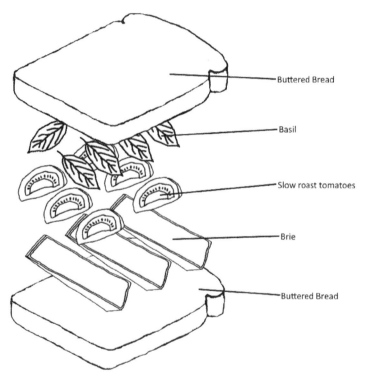

Buttered Bread

Basil

Slow roast tomatoes

Brie

Buttered Bread

Ingredients

2 slices	buttered bread
75g	brie
6pieces	slow roast tomato (component 24)
6	fresh basil leaves

N°35: Goats' Cheese, Rocket & Onion Marmalade

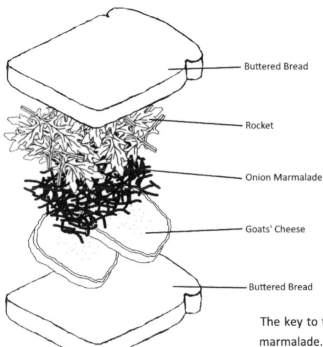

Buttered Bread

Rocket

Onion Marmalade

Goats' Cheese

Buttered Bread

The key to this is the onion marmalade. It is a slow process, but it is very simple and worth the effort. Plus once it's made it can easily be stored for a couple of weeks, due to the vinegar and sugar content.

Ingredients

2 slices	buttered bread
80g	goats' cheese (in slices)
1tsp	onion marmalade (component 25)
25g	rocket

N⁰36: Mushroom Rarebit

Rarebit, not to be confused with Rabbit. This is meat free.

Ingredients

2slices	buttered bread
50g	mature cheddar
75g	mushroom mix (component 30)
2tsp	rarebit sauce (component 43)
1dsp	crispy fried onions

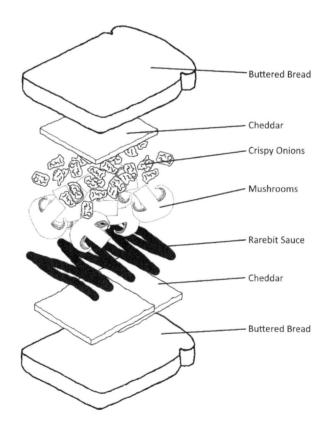

Buttered Bread

Cheddar

Crispy Onions

Mushrooms

Rarebit Sauce

Cheddar

Buttered Bread

Nº37: Butternut Squash & Ricotta

The ultimate in autumnal comfort food, also good with pumpkin instead of butternut squash (or a combination of the 2). Make sure that you use lots of ricotta.

Ingredients

2 slices	buttered bread
40g	roast butternut squash (component 31)
2tbsp	ricotta
1tsp	toasted pine nuts (component 32)
15g	baby leaf spinach

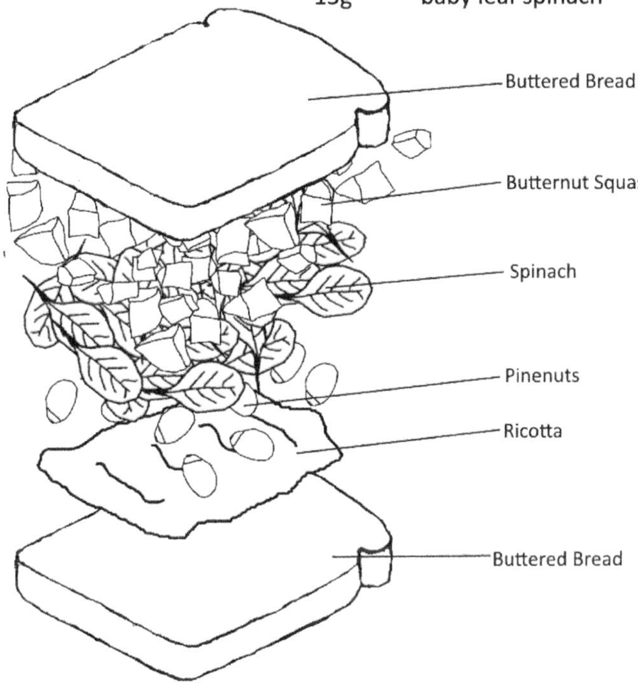

Buttered Bread

Butternut Squash

Spinach

Pinenuts

Ricotta

Buttered Bread

Nº38: Goats' Cheese, Pear and Walnut

A subtle but delicious toastie, based on the classic restaurant starter.

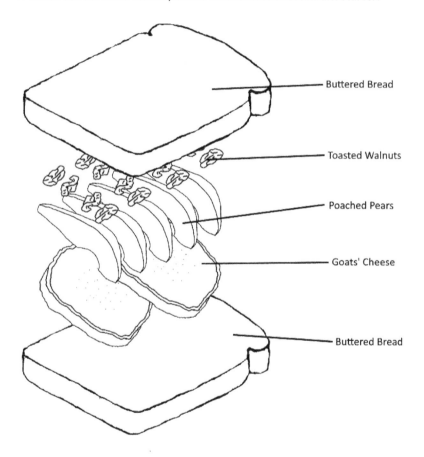

Buttered Bread

Toasted Walnuts

Poached Pears

Goats' Cheese

Buttered Bread

Ingredients

2slices	buttered bread
80g	goats cheese
½	poached pear (component 26)
4	toasted walnuts (component 27)

Nº39: Hummus and Roast Vegetables

One of our few vegan toasties. We are often asked why we don't do one with vegan cheese. The reason is that we have not found a vegan cheese that is better in a toastie than hummus. Of the vegan options we have done in the past this has always been the most popular and we think the nicest.

To make it fully vegan use margarine or rape seed oil in place of butter on the bread.

Ingredients

2slices	buttered bread
40g	plain hummus
35g	roast med veg (component 23)
1tsp	harissa

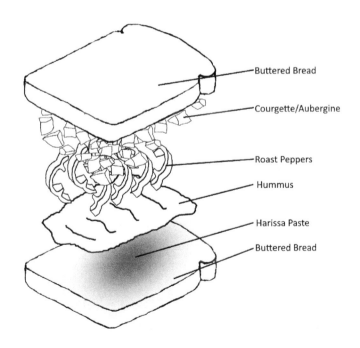

- Buttered Bread
- Courgette/Aubergine
- Roast Peppers
- Hummus
- Harissa Paste
- Buttered Bread

A5 Triple Decker Epic Toasties

The triple-decker toasties are for those with a real appetite. Originally we started with the Manwich, which was only ever meant to be sold a few times. However, it went down so well and it has such a loyal following that it has become a regular feature of our menu. We have experimented with the form so the Manwich has offspring and 4 of them are included here along with the original epic toastie.

All of the epics are based around the same idea; cook 2 toasties, load something tasty on to toastie number 1 add cheese and then stick toastie 2 on top before pressing together. These can only be made in a panini-style toastie machine due to their ridiculous size. Each recipe has the first (left) and second (right) presses separted.

Nº40: The Manwich

One of our award winning toasties, this won "Best Toasted Sandwich" at the 2015 Cafelife awards. Years after we sold it for the first time it is still my favourite item on the menu. This toastie is comprised of a "Ham and Cheese" (No1) top and a "Manwich Base".

Make sure to season the steak then slice it nice and thin across the grain for a better eating experience.

When it comes to hot sauce; in this recipe don't use anything outraguously hot. The hot sauce is a seasoning here and it shouldn't blow your head off. I like Pip's "La Bocca del Diablo" best, but any medium strength sauce will do.

Ingredients

4slices	buttered bread
60g	cheddar
35g	ham
2slices	pastrami
4 slices	chorizo
2	streaky bacon rashers
6oz	steak
25g	Monterey Jack
50g	mozzarella
¼	caramelised onion (component 33)
½tsp	garlic puree
½tsp	hot sauce

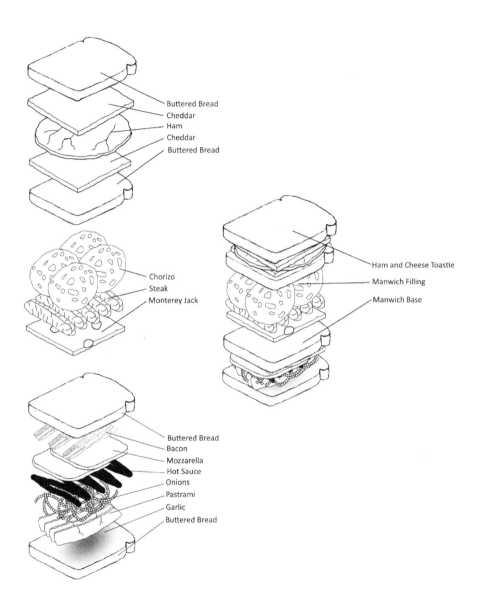

Buttered Bread
Cheddar
Ham
Cheddar
Buttered Bread

Chorizo
Steak
Monterey Jack

Ham and Cheese Toastie
Manwich Filling
Manwich Base

Buttered Bread
Bacon
Mozzarella
Hot Sauce
Onions
Pastrami
Garlic
Buttered Bread

Nº41: Old Macdonald

This is called the Old Macdonald as it has so many different animals. It was also named The Farmyard Massacre by a group of customers known to us as The Rolls-Royce Regulars.

This might be the most dense sandwich we have ever created. It's good with a pickle on the side to cut through the richness of the meat. If you can't get gooseberry chutney then any sharp pickle will do.

The best way to heat up the pork is to flambé it in some booze. If you can't be bothered then stick it in the magic box (microwave) instead.

Ingredients

4 slices	buttered bread
50g	braised lamb (component 7)
25g	roast beef (component 5)
65g	pulled pork (component 2)
30g	confit duck (component 14)
50g	roast chicken (component 4)
50g	gouda
50g	mozzarella
50g	cheddar
½tsp	English mustard
1tsp	gooseberry chutney
Pinch	salt
25ml	whiskey or brandy

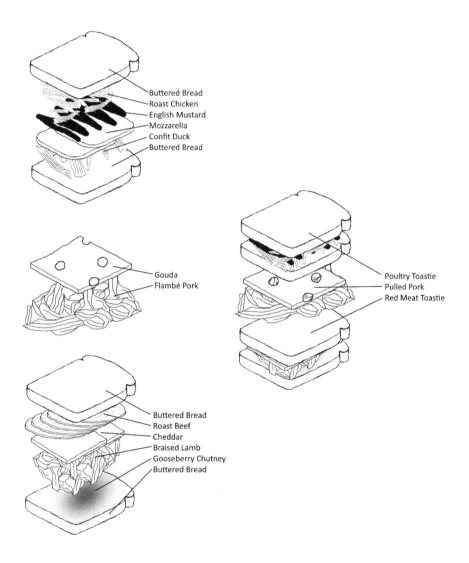

Buttered Bread
Roast Chicken
English Mustard
Mozzarella
Confit Duck
Buttered Bread

Gouda
Flambé Pork

Poultry Toastie
Pulled Pork
Red Meat Toastie

Buttered Bread
Roast Beef
Cheddar
Braised Lamb
Gooseberry Chutney
Buttered Bread

Nº42: Great Balls of Fire

This is what happens when a Manwich gets a bit frisky with a meatball sub. Again like the Manwich, half of this is another sandwich featuered earlier in the book, in this case it is the "Chorizo and Jalapeno" (No 12).

The point of this toasted sandwich was to produce a tasty HOT toastie. When we sell this we have a second type of extra spicy hot sauce available so people can choose their own level of heat. This is therefore a matter for you to decide... use whichever hot sauce you think you can handle.

Ingredients

4 slices	buttered bread
50g	mozzarella
6 slices	chorizo (thin sliced)
6pieces	jalapeños (thick sliced)
½tsp	garlic puree
6	mini meat balls (component 13)
1tbsp	marinara sauce (component 44)
25g	parmesan (grated)
9slices	pepperoni (1mm slices)
1	roasted peppers
1tsp	hot sauce
50g	cheddar

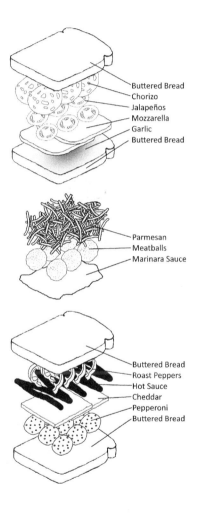

Buttered Bread
Chorizo
Jalapeños
Mozzarella
Garlic
Buttered Bread

Parmesan
Meatballs
Marinara Sauce

Buttered Bread
Roast Peppers
Hot Sauce
Cheddar
Pepperoni
Buttered Bread

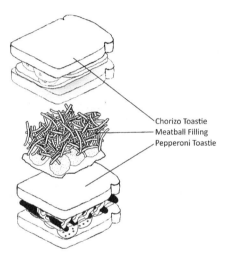

Chorizo Toastie
Meatball Filling
Pepperoni Toastie

Nº43: The Kraken

The idea behind this toastie was to create the ultimate fish finger sandwich. You can make your own fish fingers and they will be better than bought ones, but they take time and a lot of effort.

This differs from other epic toasties as both toasties are the same.

Ingredients

4 slices	buttered bread
2tsp	pickled cockles
2tsp	tartare sauce
90g	cold water prawns
100g	edam
30g	watercress
30g	cheddar
½	beef tomato (thick sliced)
3	fish fingers

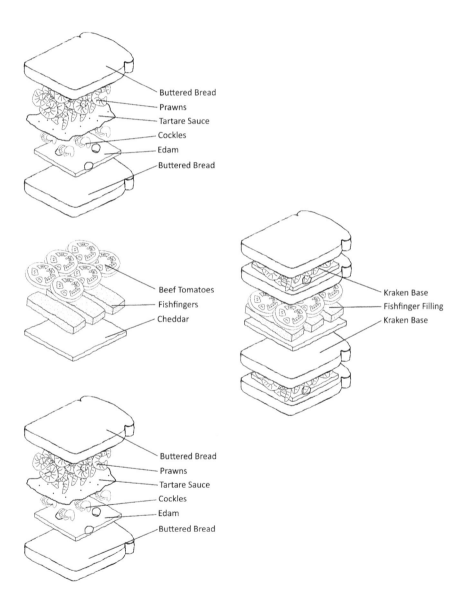

Buttered Bread
Prawns
Tartare Sauce
Cockles
Edam
Buttered Bread

Beef Tomatoes
Fishfingers
Cheddar

Kraken Base
Fishfinger Filling
Kraken Base

Buttered Bread
Prawns
Tartare Sauce
Cockles
Edam
Buttered Bread

N°44: The Candy Manwich

Credit must go to the "Rolls Royce Regulars" for coming up with the name and then challenging us to make this most twisted of toasties. It's delicious… just don't ask for a calorie count. This toastie has been featured on TV and Simon Rimmer said "it's actually very good". I'll take the compliment; even if it's a bit back handed.

Be warned; this toastie makes a mess of the press due the amount of sugar that leaks out. Make sure to wipe the heating plates afterwards or risk setting off the smoke alarm next time you make a ham and cheese. Wipe down with a damp sponge while the press is still warm and the sugar should come straight off.

I think blackcurrants are best in this sandwich. However, they are hard to get hold of and blueberries will suffice. Passion fruit curd is annoying to find ready made as well, but we have discovered that almost all National Trust properties sell it in the attached shop.

And yes the middle is a deep fried Mars Bar (thank you to Nick for suggesting that one).

<u>Ingredients</u>

4 slices	buttered bread
3	candy bacon rashers (component 3)
9	blackcurrants
1tbsp	mini marsh mallows
1tsp	passion fruit curd
66g	carnation caramel/toffee sauce (component 46)
1	banana (1.5cm slices)
1	deep-fried-Mars-bar (component 45)

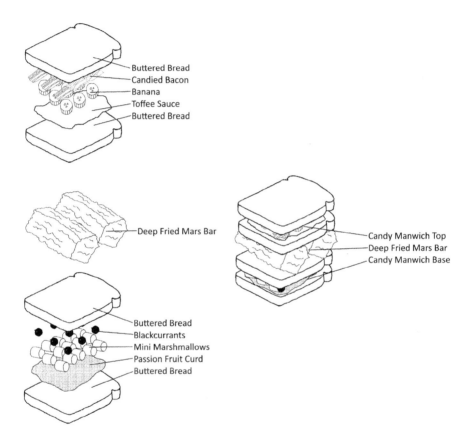

Buttered Bread
Candied Bacon
Banana
Toffee Sauce
Buttered Bread

Deep Fried Mars Bar

Candy Manwich Top
Deep Fried Mars Bar
Candy Manwich Base

Buttered Bread
Blackcurrants
Mini Marshmallows
Passion Fruit Curd
Buttered Bread

A6 Dessert Toasties

In The Jabberwocky we have always sold sweet toasties. For a reason that I have never been able to adequately explain, the public are sceptical. This is a surprise as toasties are effectively 2 pieces of toast stuck together. Everyone is happy to eat jam or chocolate spread on toast, but call it a toastie and people get scared. This is a shame for 2 reasons. Firstly people always come back for more once they have tried our sweet options. Secondly, because some our best creations are desserts. Please give these a try when you have finally got sick of eating melted cheese.

Also a warning; if you think that cheese inside a toastie can get hot, wait until you have tried a dessert toastie. All of my worst burns have come from sweet, not from the cheesy options.

Nº45:Banoffee

Our original sweet toastie. Simple, delicious and credit must go to my Mum for the idea. To begin with, this was chocolate and banana, which was nice, but not as good as this and this has the spark of originallity that we love.

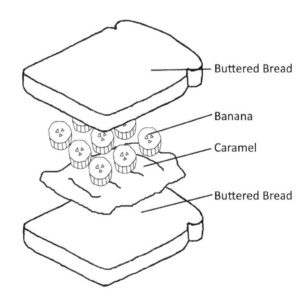

Buttered Bread

Banana

Caramel

Buttered Bread

Ingredients

2slices	buttered bread
½	banana (sliced)
66g	Carnation caramel (6th of a can) (component 46)

Nº46: Rocky Road

Based on the quintessential fridge cake. There is no agreement about what goes in a rocky road, so this is our version. Just leave out whatever you don't like, but no I won't pick out the raisins for you.

It is important to make the filling into the rocky road mix before using (otherwise the filling will fallout everywhere and burn to the toastie press).

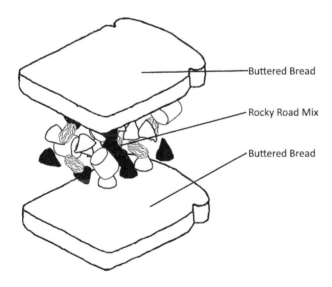

Buttered Bread

Rocky Road Mix

Buttered Bread

Ingredients

2slices	buttered bread
2tbsp	rocky road mix (component 47)

Nº47: Rhubarb and Custard

A lovely combination of sweet custard and sour rhubarb. This toastie is only OK on normal bread, but heavenly on brioche. Due to the high level of sugar in brioche it will burn much faster than normal bread. So if you can, turn your toastie press down.

Make the custard in advance and chill before using in the toatie.

Ingredients

2slices	buttered brioche
1tbsp	custard (component 49)
6	cooked rhubarb (component 48)

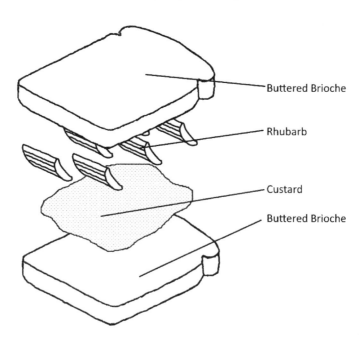

Buttered Brioche

Rhubarb

Custard

Buttered Brioche

Nº48: Raspberry and Orange

Really simple to make, but so good. Make life easy: don't make orange curd, just buy it. If you can't get orange, then curd lemon is also good here, just not quite as great. The number of raspberries sounds like we are being mean, but too many and they are all you can taste.

Ingredients

2slices	buttered brioche
3tsp	orange curd
6	large raspberries

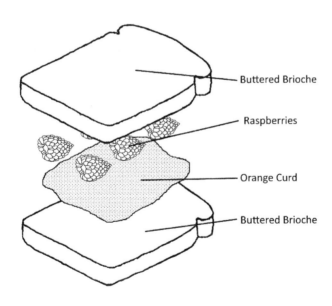

Buttered Brioche

Raspberries

Orange Curd

Buttered Brioche

Nº49: Blackberry and Apple

Another classic combination given the toastie-treatment. Get out and pick the blackberries; they are way better than farmed ones, free and grow everywhere. This is also nice if you include a little cooked crumble topping or some smashed up biscuits.

Ingredients

2slices	buttered brioche
6	blackberries
1tbsp	custard (component 49)
1tbsp	apple sauce (component 39)

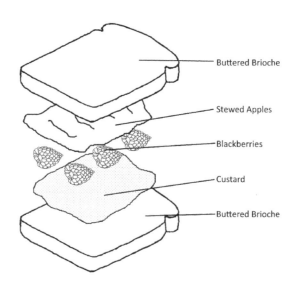

Buttered Brioche

Stewed Apples

Blackberries

Custard

Buttered Brioche

Nº50: Mincepie Toastie

Trust us on this one and try it. This is one of our most requested and asked after toasties. Every year from October onward people will be asking when it's back. Even if you don't like it in a toastie the mincemeat is an old family recipe and is so much better than supermarket versions.

To go with this you need some brandy butter to dip into for a perfect indulgent seasonal snack.

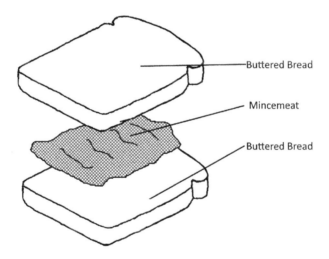

Buttered Bread

Mincemeat

Buttered Bread

Ingredients

2slices   buttered bread
1tbsp   mincemeat (component 50)
1tbsp   brandy butter (component 51)

Section B: Component Instructions

Toasties are easy to make and that is one of the reasons they are the best food in the world. However, to make a truly spectacular toasted sandwich you have to do some real cooking first.

This section contains all the recipes for the components that cannot (or should not) be bought easily in shops. During the last decade we have relentlessly tested our versions against readymade equivalents. In some cases we have found that it is better to buy components (e.g. ham) because they taste better or the effort involved is just too great, but most are best when cooked fresh. For example you can buy roast chicken in any supermarket, but it's never going to be as tasty as the bird you have cooked at home.

All recipes are given in metric and most do not need lots of specialist equipment. It is worth investing in a food probe thermometer as this will make your meat taste better and make all your cooking safer to eat.

Salt and pepper quantities are not given in most recipes as they are almost always done to taste. If you are not used to doing this, just eat a little of the component, add salt and pepper and sample again. Repeat this until it tastes fantastic. Anytime a recipe calls for "seasoning" it means salt and pepper unless otherwise stated.

Component 1
Spreadable Butter

The first component has to be spreadable butter. It doesn't fit into any other category but is used in every single recipe. In section C there is more info about alternatives to this ingredient (page 133). Remember that with a toastie butter always goes on the outside!

This can be made by hand, but is a lot easier on an electric mixer, so if you don't own one you might want to give this a miss. Once it's set it should be a good consistency to spread directly from the fridge.

Make sure all the oil is not too cold or it will cause the butter to form lumps.

Makes: 50 toasties

      250g   salted butter

      250ml rapeseed oil (or sunflower)

1. Soften butter in the microwave
2. Cream the butter until very white, soft and fluffy
3. Turn speed down and add 50ml oil. Allow this to incorporate fully
4. Add the rest of the oil slowly and allow to fully mix
5. Set in the fridge for 24 hours.

B1: Meat Components

Component 2
Pulled Pork

This is actually a "Bo Saam Pork" recipe, but in our experience this makes the tastiest pulled pork (if you don't own a smoker). Plus it has an amazing salty-sweet crust that isn't used in the toastie so it is just for the chef to enjoy.

2kg	shoulder of pork boned and rolled
3tbsp	salt
3tbsp	white sugar
1tbsp	demerara sugar
1tsp	salt

1. Place the pork in a baking tray.
2. Mix white sugar and salt together and rub all over the meat.
3. Cover the meat and refrigerate overnight. This will draw out water.
4. Poor away any liquid or salt/sugar that has pooled around the pork.
5. Put the pork shoulder, fat-side up, uncovered into a pre-heated oven at 150ºC.
6. Baste with the fat that is rendered every hour.
7. Roast for 4-7 hours depending on the amount of pork and the oven. When cooked it will fall apart.
8. Stop here for toastie meat. Let the meat cool and pull it apart discarding the fat and sinew. The following instructions are for the same dish if wish to eat the meat as a joint or as Bo Saam pork.
9. Rest the meat at room temperature for 30 mins.
10. Turn the oven up as high as it will go.
11. Mix the brown sugar and 1 tsp salt together and rub into the outside of the pork.
12. Place the pork in the middle of the hot oven until the sugar has caramelised then eat.

Component 3
Candied Bacon

Delicious and addicitive...beware of the maple syrup burning to the baking tray as it's a devil to remove.

This recipe is for 3 rashers, but doing a full baking tray works better.

3	streaky bacon rashers
30ml	maple syrup (10 ml per bacon rasher)

1. Lay the bacon flat on a baking tray.
2. Using a pastry brush, paint the bacon with a liberal amount of maple syrup.
3. Put into a hot oven (200ºC) for 10 mins.
4. Re paint with maple syrup.
5. Bake for another 15 mins or until it has started to caramelise.
6. Remove from the oven and chop into chunks while the bacon is still warm.

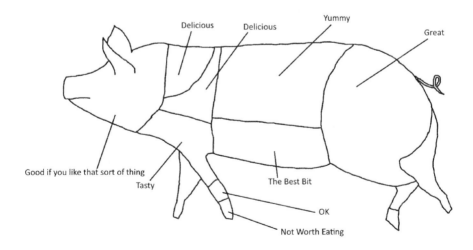

Component 4
Roast Chicken

This recipe makes around 10-15 toasties worth of chicken depending on the size of the bird used.

1	large chicken
1	onion
2	garlic
1tbsp	olive oil
	salt and pepper
50ml	white wine

1. Quarter the onion and stuff into the cavity along with 2 cloves of garlic.
2. Rub the skin of the bird with olive oil and then season generously.
3. Place on a large baking tray.
4. Cook in a pre-heated oven @ 200°C for 45 mins. For best results invest in a food thermometer and cook the chicken until the minimum temperature reached anywhere in the meat is 75°C. This will give you safe and juicy chicken every time.
5. Cool, with the skin on.
6. Strip the meat from the bones and place in a large container. Taste the meat and season if required. Remember to mix the salt and pepper thoroughly through the meat.
7. Reserve any juices and fat that have rendered out during cooking.
8. De-glaze the roasting dish with white wine.
9. Mix the juices and white wine. Take off the top layer of fat.
10. Pour the juices over the meat and chill for 24 hours. During this time the meat will draw in some of the liquid, so it will become more juicy and tender as well as absorbing extra flavour.

Component 5
Roast Beef

1kg   topside of beef

      salt and pepper

      oil

1. Rub the meat with a little oil. This will allow the salt and pepper to stick to the outside of the meat.
2. Season the meat HEAVILY with salt and pepper.
3. Place on a trivet on a baking tray.
4. Roast in pre-heated oven @ 180°C for 45mins. Or use a food thermometer and look for a core temperature of 60°C for delicious pink beef.
5. Remove from the oven and cool for 60mins.
6. Tightly and thoroughly wrap piece of beef in cling film.
7. Chill for 24 hours.
8. Slice the beef as thinly as you can. This is much easier once the beef is cooled to fridge temperature. Remember to go across the grain of the meat for a more pleasant eating experience.

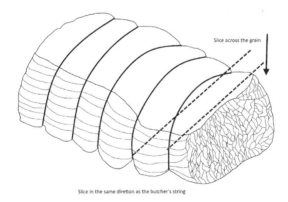

Slice in the same diretion as the butcher's string

Component 6
Braised Venison

This is a slow cook recipe so get the cheapest cut you can. The cheaper cuts have the most flavour, but do need a slow, gentle cook to avoid it being chewy.

2kg	venison (shoulder, shank or haunch)
2	white onions
4	carrots
4	celery
6	garlic cloves
2	leek
1tsp	mixed herbs
	salt and pepper
250ml	red wine
2l	stock (chicken or vegetable)

1. Peel and roughly chop the vegetables.
2. Lay veg in a large oven proof container and add herbs and a generous amount of seasoning.
3. Lay venison on top.
4. Add red wine, then top up with stock until the meat is nearly submerged.
5. Cook the meat @ 135°C for 8 hours or until soft.
6. Remove from oven and allow to cool.
7. Remove the meat from the liquid and pull apart with your hands. Remove any fat or connective tissue, while retaining meat in a container.
8. Taste the meat. This is the time to add extra seasoning if required
9. Strain the liquid to remove the vegetables
10. Pour cooking liquid onto the seasoned meat until is half way to the level of the top of the meat. Only use the cooking liquid, not the fat for this. Mix the meat and juices.
11. Seal container and place it in the fridge for 12 hours to cool thoroughly. During this time the meat will also draw up some of the liquid making it juicier and more tender.

Component 7
Braised Lamb

1	shoulder of lamb, boned and rolled
1	white onion
2	carrots
3	celery
4	garlic cloves
1	leek
2tsp	dried mint
	salt and pepper
150ml	red wine
1l	stock

1. Peel and roughly chop the vegetables.
2. Lay veg in a large oven proof container and add herbs and plenty of seasoning
3. Lay lamb on top.
4. Add red wine, then add stock until the meat is submerged.
5. Cook @ 135°C for 8 hours or until meat is very soft (a spoon should be able to cut it).
6. Remove from oven and allow to cool.
7. Remove the meat from the liquid and pull apart with your hands. Remove any fat or connective tissue, while retaining meat in a container.
8. Taste the meat. This is the time to add extra seasoning if required.
9. Strain the liquid to remove the vegetables.
10. Pour cooking liquid onto the seasoned meat until is NEARLY submerged. Only use the cooking liquid not the fat for this.
11. Seal container and place it in the fridge for 12 hours to cool thoroughly. During this time the meat will also draw up some of the liquid so it will become juicier and more tender. Most fat will rise to the surface, which should be scraped off and disposed of before using the meat.

Component 8
Lamb Koftas

250g	lamb mince (mutton mince is even better)
1tsp	garlic puree
¾tsp	salt
1tsp	turmeric
1tsp	cumin
¼tsp	black pepper
¼tsp	chilli powder
¼tsp	ginger
½tsp	fenugreek
1tsp	fennel seeds
1tsp	coriander leaf
4drops	Tabasco

1. Mix all the ingredients. If the mix is wet add a handful of breadcrumbs.
2. Shape into koftas (thin sausage shapes). The mix will make 15 small koftas (or 8 large kofta for a non toastie meal).
   Approximately 15g for toastie size Kofta and 40g for koftas for a meal.
3. Cook in a little oil in a frying pan for 5 mins, turning occasionally until thoroughly cooked.

Component 9
Roast Turkey

1	turkey
2	white onions
3	garlic cloves
½pt	chicken stock
	salt and pepper

1. Place the bird in a deep roasting dish.
2. Chop 2 onions into quarters and smash a couple of garlic cloves. Stuff these into the turkey.
3. Oil and season the skin with salt and pepper.
4. Put ½ pint of chicken stock around the turkey.
5. Wrap the whole thing in tin foil.
6. Cook in a pre-heated oven (180°C).
7. After 90 mins turn the bird upside down so the breasts are in the liquid.
8. Roast until the thickest part reaches 75°C.
9. Leave to cool in the juices.
10. Pull apart the meat and season with salt and pepper. Then pour over the juices (not the fat) and chill for 24 hours.

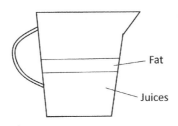

Fat

Juices

Component 10
Smoked Pigeon

For this I recommend you use a barrel barbeque or any other type. Smoking can be done indoors, but it is unlikely to ingratiate you with whomever you live with, so best done in the garden.

You need about 1 breast per toastie, but if you are going to the effort of smoking meat you might as well do a whole batch at the same time. This is a really easy, quick way of hot smoking some meat.

> pigeon breast (boned and skinned)
> rosemary/thyme (3-4 branches of each)
> loose earl grey tea
> olive oil
> salt and pepper

1. Light the barbeque in the normal way.
2. Toss the pigeon in a little oil (drain off any excess) and season well.
3. Once the charcoal is ready to cook on, throw the herbs and tea directly onto the coals.
4. Put the pigeon on the grill and close the lid (open as little as possible from now on).
5. Smoke for 10-15mins (turn after 5mins) or until the meat is cooked through. A hint of pink is perfect.
6. Allow to cool and slice thinly along the length of the breasts.

Component 11
Roast Pheasant

Brace   pheasant (2)

2 sprigs rosemary

1   onion

4   garlic cloves

         olive oil

         salt and pepper

         white wine

1. Quarter the onion and stuff ½ into each bird along with 2 cloves of garlic and a rosemary sprig.
2. Rub the skin of each bird with olive oil and then generously with salt and pepper.
3. Place on a large baking tray.
4. Cook in a pre-heated oven @ 200°C for 30 mins. For the best results invest in a food thermometer and cook the pheasant until the minimum temperature reached anywhere in the meat is 75°C. This will give you safe and juicy meat every time.
5. Cool with the skin on.
6. Strip the meat from the bones and place in a large container. Taste the meat and add salt and pepper if required. Remember to mix the salt and pepper thoroughly through the meat.
7. Reserve any juices and fat that have rendered out during cooking
8. De-glaze the roasting dish with white wine.
9. Mix the any roasting juices and white wine. Take off the top layer of fat
10. Pour the juices over the meat and chill for 24 hours.

Alternatively, if you can get them, pheasant breasts can be used by cooking in a frying pan over medium heat for about 8mins. Season with salt and pepper first and turn them regularly (just chill and slice after cooking).

Component 12 Braised Buffalo

2kg	brisket of water buffalo
2	white onions
4	carrots
4	celery
6	garlic
2	leek
1tsp	mixed herbs
250ml	red wine
2l	stock (chicken)
	salt and pepper

1. Peel and roughly chop vegetables.
2. Lay veg in a large oven proof container and add herbs and generous amount of salt and pepper.
3. Lay meat on top.
4. Add red wine, thenpour on stock until the meat just submerged. Do not use beef stock as this will drown out the unique taste of the buffalo.
5. Cook @ 135°C for 8 hours or until meat is very soft (if spoon easily cuts the meat, it is ready).
6. Remove from the oven and allow to cool.
7. Remove the meat from the liquid and pull apart with your hands. Remove any fat or connective tissue, while retaining meat in a container
8. Taste the meat. This is the time to add extra seasoning if required
9. Strain the liquid to remove the vegetables
10. Pour cooking liquid onto the seasoned meat until is NEARLY submerged. Only use the cooking liquid not the fat for this. Mix the juices and meat.
11. Seal container and place it in the fridge for 12 hours to cool thoroughly.

Component 13
Meatballs

500g	minced beef (or pork)
1	onion (pureed)
1dsp	garlic puree
1	egg
2tsp	paprika
½tsp	cayenne
½tsp	chilli powder
1tsp	dried coriander
2 slices	bread crumbs (you may not need all of these)

1. Mix together all the ingredients (except the bread crumbs).
2. Once thoroughly mixed add bread crumbs until you have a mix that can be formed into balls.
3. Form the meat into balls 2cm in diameter.
4. Refrigerate for 2 hours so they are firm before cooking.
5. Cook in a frying pan with a little butter for about 5 mins turning regularly.

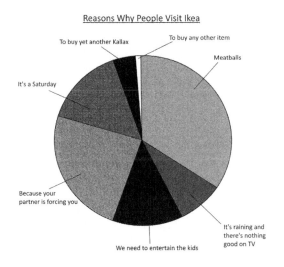

Reasons Why People Visit Ikea

Component 14
Confit Duck

This recipe will make a lot of duck, but it is hard to do a very small amount of confit duck and have it cook properly.

4	duck legs
2tbsp	salt
80g	fresh thyme
½l	duck fat (pork fat or olive oil can be substituted)
2	bay leaves
½tsp	black pepper

1. Toss the duck legs in the salt and chill for 24 hours. This will help to remove as much water as possible.
2. Brush off the salt and discard along with any liquid that has collected.
3. Melt the duck fat (pork fat or olive oil can also be used) in a large sauce pan, with the thyme, garlic, pepper and bay leaves.
4. Add the duck legs to the fat so the bones stick up.
5. Cook gently for about 2 hours. When the bones can be easily pulled out of the meat they are ready.
6. Allow to cool.
7. Strip the meat off the bones.
8. Strain the fat through a fine sieve, add 2tbsp to the meat and mix well. Taste and season with salt and pepper if required.
9. Chill in the fridge for 24 hours.
10. Alternatively you can cover the meat with fat entirely for meat that will remain fresh and tasty for 2 weeks in the fridge.

B2 Seafood & Fish Components

Component 15
Tuna Mayo

240g	drained tuna chunks
Dash	Worcestershire sauce
½tsp	fresh dill – finely chopped
1dsp	mayo
1tsp	grated parmesan
	salt and pepper

1. Drain the tuna as much as possible.
2. In a bowl, mix all the ingredients with the tuna and salt and pepper to taste.

Component 16
Dressed Crab

500g	mixed brown and white crab meat
15ml	lemon juice
1tsp	Dijon mustard
	salt and pepper

Mix, but be gentle so you do not break apart the crab meat.

Component 17
Poached Lobster

The best lobsters are still alive when you buy them, but it is unnecessarily cruel to cook them while still alive. Best practise is to chill them in a freezer for about 20mins (this will put them into a coma), then cut through the head with a sharp knife in a single cut (see below).

1kg	fresh lobster
1L	water
250ml	white wine
1	onion
2	garlic cloves
1	stick of celery
1	leek
50g	parsley
1tsp	salt
¼tsp	pepper

1. Put all the ingredients in a stock pot and bring to the boil for 5 mins.
2. Turn down to a gentle simmer.
3. Add the dead lobster and poach (do not boil) for 18mins.
4. Remove from the water and cool.
5. Pick out all the meat and reserve. The meat can be found in the claws and tail (to a lesser extent the legs). The rest of the lobster is not good to eat, but shell will make lovely stock.

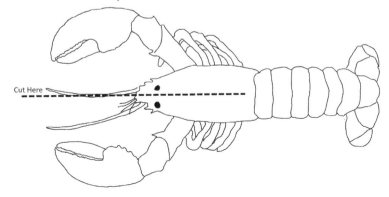

Cut Here

Component 18
Scallops

4	queen scallops
15g	butter
1	lemon
	salt and pepper

1. Heat a little butter in a frying pan.
2. Add the scallops and season with salt, pepper and lemon juice.
3. Cook scallops for about 1 min on each side (until golden).

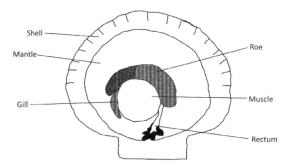

Apparently the entire scallop can be eaten. However, normally just the muscle is used. The roe is nice if you like similar seafood items.

B3 Vegetable & Cheese Components

Component 19
Creamed Feta

200g   feta cheese
250g   cream cheese
Pinch pepper

1. Roughly dice the feta.
2. Mix on an electric mixer on high speed to break it apart more.
3. Add pepper.
4. Add cream cheese and beat for 2 mins.
5. Scrape the bottom of the mixer bowl (the feta has a tendency to stick to the bottom of the bowl and so not be incorporated properly) and re-mix. This step may have to be repeated.

Component 20
Stilton Pâté

150g   stilton
150g   cashel blue
150g   cream cheese
       salt and pepper to taste

1. Roughly dice the stilton.
2. Beat on an electric mixer.
3. Add the roughly chopped cashel and beat into a sticky mess.
4. Add cream cheese and beat, until combined (about 5 minutes).
5. Scrape the bottom of the mixer bowl and re-mix.
6. Taste and season with salt and pepper if needed.

Component 21
Roast Shallot

The best shallots to use for this recipe are "banana" shallots as they are bigger and therefore involve less effort. White onions can be substituted

4	banana shallots
2tbsp	rape seed oil
	salt and pepper

1. Cut the tops and roots off the shallots.
2. Peel the shallots, but keep them whole.
3. Cut in half length ways.
4. Slice each into about 4 pieces through the root stem.
5. Toss the shallots in olive or rape seed oil.
6. Season generously with salt and black pepper.
7. Lay them out in a roasting dish.
8. Roat for 20 mins @200ºC or until golden brown and soft.

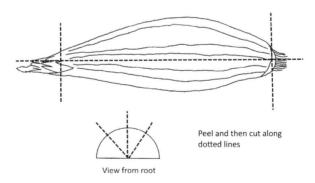

Peel and then cut along dotted lines

View from root

Component 22
Roast Peppers

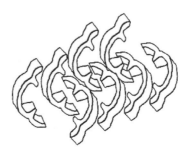

An alternative is to buy pre-roasted tinned peppers. If you find the right brand they are perfect for toasties and involve a lot less effort. Tinned peppers, tend to be very wet so make sure that you remove as much moisture as possible before they go into a toastie, if you are using them.

It is pretty hard to do fewer than 3 peppers as they tend to burn if you don't have enough peppers on the baking tray.

The traditional method is to skin the peppers before cooking. To do this hold them in a flame and the skin will blister and burn. It can then be rubbed off under cold water. It takes a lot of effort and is not nessecary for use in a toastie. I quite like the texture of cooked pepper skin, which is also a good source of fibre.

3	red pepper
	Salt and pepper
2tsp	olive oil

1. Core the peppers and slice length ways into 5mm wide slices.
2. Coat the peppers with olive oil and season with salt and pepper.
3. Lay out on a baking tray.
4. Roast at 180°C for 12 mins, or until soft and beginning to colour.

Component 23 Roast Mediterranean Vegetables

This recipe makes approximately 6 portions of roast vegetables.

2	peppers 1cm³ dice (1 red, 1 yellow)
1	courgette 1cm³ dice
1	aubergine 1cm³ dice
½	onion 1cm³ dice
2tbsp	olive oil
2	garlic cloves (chopped)

1. Toss the vegetables in olive oil.
2. Spread over a large roasting tin and season well with salt and pepper.
3. Roast for 20mins @180°C.

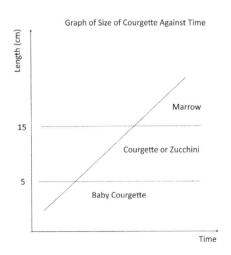

Component 24
Slow Roast Tomatoes

There is a minimum amount of tomatoes that can be roasted. If too few are on the tray they will burn before they roast properly. Below is a rough guide to time and temperature: the lower and slower they are cooked; the better they are. It may take a little experimenting to get it right in your oven.

When roasting; use a shallow roasting tray. A deep one will keep too much of the moisture in with the tomatoes and they will go sloppy during cooking.

Too much garlic is the way to go on this recipe, Flic calls this the Garlic Supernova (in a good way).

Approximately 10 portions (1 standard roasting tray)

8	fresh vine ripe tomatoes
1tsp	mixed herbs
1tbsp	olive oil
2tsp	garlic puree
	salt and pepper

1. Cut each tomato in to 8 wedge shaped pieces.
2. Mix all the ingredients so the tomatoes are evenly coated in the other components.
3. Spread onto a baking tray so they do not overlap.
4. Roast @130°C for 2½ hours.

Component 25
Onion Marmalade

This will make a lot of onion marmalade, but because of the vinegar and sugar it keeps for weeks in the fridge. It is great on a cheese sandwich or give it to someone who loves pickle.

> 1kg   red onions (thinly sliced)
> 300ml balsamic vinegar
> 115g   demerara sugar
>   salt and pepper

1. Sweat the red onions in a sauce pan on a gentle heat in a little oil for 15 mins or until soft.
2. Add salt and pepper and balsamic vinegar.
3. Bring to a gentle simmer.
4. Stir occasionally until the liquid has almost all be evaporated.
5. Turn up the heat and add the sugar.
6. More liquid should come out of the onions (be careful not to burn the mixture from this point onwards).
7. Boil and stir until the remaining liquid is thick and gloopy.
8. Cool and store in the fridge.

Component 26 Poached Pears

250ml	white wine
250ml	water
½tsp	nutmeg
½tsp	cloves
1	cinnamon stick
½	orange
100g	sugar
3	pears

1. Mix the spices, orange, sugar, wine and water ina large pan and bring to a gentle simmer.
2. Meanwhile peel the pears.
3. Put the pears into the poaching liquid. They should be totally submergered.
4. Cook for about 20mins (this will vary depending how many pears you are cooking and how ripe they are). They are cooked when tender all the way through.
5. Remove from the liquid and allow to cool.
6. Halve and core the pears before slicing into pieces for use.

Component 27
Toasted Walnuts

8   walnut halves

1. Chop each walnut half into 4 pieces.
2. Heat a dry frying pan (medium heat).
3. Add the walnut pieces and toast in the dry frying pan – keep them moving to avoid burning.
4. Cook until they have a golden colour.

Component 28
Cauliflower

1. Cut off the florets
2. Blanch in boiling water for 1 min
3. Refresh in cold water
4. Cut into thick slices.

Refresh

This means empty out the boiling water then run a cold tap into the pan with the vegetables. The cauliflower will stay in the pan while the pan over flows. Keep the water running until the veg has cooled down. This is one of the most efficient and quickest ways to stop the cooking process.

Blanch

"To cook without colour". The water must be at a rolling boil and you are looking to cook the item for a short time, without losing any of the natural colour.

Component 29 Artichoke and Roast Garlic Puree

2	garlic bulbs
400g	tinned artichoke hearts (drained)
1tsp	horseradish sauce
1tsp	lemon juice
	salt and pepper

1. Cut the top off the garlic bulb and place cut side down on to a well oil baking tray.
2. Roast in the oven at 140°C until the garlic has become soft.
3. Squeeze the garlic into a food processor (discard the skin).
4. Add the other ingredients and blitz until a thick puree is formed.

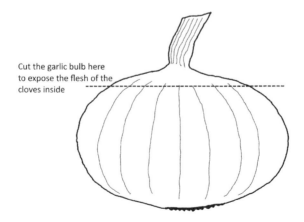

Cut the garlic bulb here to expose the flesh of the cloves inside

Component 30
Mushroom Mix

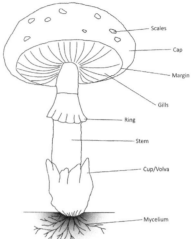

300g	chestnut mushrooms
300g	oyster mushrooms
50g	dried porchini mushrooms

1. Rehydrate the porchini mushrooms as directed on the pack. Reserve the liquor.
2. Slice the oyster and chestnut mushrooms.
3. Fry the fresh mushrooms in butter and salt & pepper until thoroughly cooked.
4. Remove from the pan and drain any liquid.
5. Combine the pochini liquor with the mushroom liquid and return to the pan.
6. Boil the liquid until it is the consistency of treacle and add it to the fried mushrooms and the rehydrated porchini.
7. Mix well.

Component 31 Roast Butternut Squash

1	butternut squash (1cm³ dice)
80g	fresh sage
2tbsp	olive oil
	salt and pepper

1. Peel, de-seed and dice the butternut squash.
2. Roughly chop the sage.
3. Mix all the ingredients in a large bowl so the butternut is well coated in oil and herbs.
4. Spread onto a baking tray.
5. Roast for 20mins at 180°C or until golden and soft.

Component 32 Toasted Pine Nuts

Toasting pine nuts will concentrate the flavour and add a caramel zing to the toastie or just snack on them.

1. Heat a frying pan on medium heat. Do not add oil.
2. Add a handful of pine nuts and a little salt.
3. Keep the pine nuts moving around the pan to avoid burning.
4. Cook until they are golden brown.

Component 33
Caramelised Onions

Not all onions need the sugar adding. Some will have enough natural sugar to caramelise without adding extra.

> 1   onion (sliced)
>
> 1tbsp rape seed oil
>
> 1tsp   sugar

1. Fry the onion in the oil over a medium heat until cooked.
2. Turn the heat up to add a little colour to the onions.
3. Add the sugar and cook until dark caramel colour (be careful not to burn the sugar).

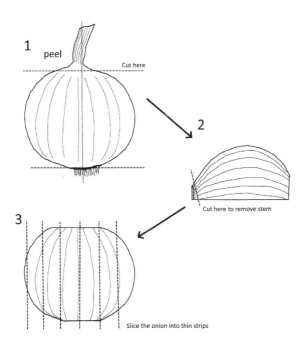

Component 34
Egg Mayo

This egg mayo is for toastie use and will not make a good egg and cress sandwich as it has so little mayo. The mayonnaise is just enough to hold the mixture together.

Below it says to grate the egg (yes, on a cheese grater). This is the best way to make a large amount egg mayo and results in a good size of egg chunk. However, you can just smash it with a fork if you would rather. Grating an egg sounds weird, but it works. Just do not use an electric grater, believe me when I say: I have tried and you should not.

1	egg
8g	mayonnaise
	salt and pepper

1. Boil egg for 8mins.
2. Refresh (see component 28).
3. Peel and grate the egg.
4. Add mayo and Salt and pepper.

Egg Freshness Test

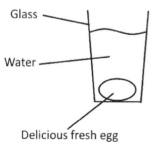
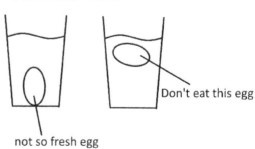

Glass

Water

Delicious fresh egg

not so fresh egg

Don't eat this egg

B4 Sauce Components

Component 35
Cumberland Sauce

200ml   port
1   orange (juice and zest)
2tbsp   redcurrant jelly

1.   Put all the ingredients into a sauce pan.
2.   Bring to a gentle simmer and let it reduce to half the volume.
3.   Chill.

This recipe relies on reducing the volume by half. The easiest way to measure this is using a ruler. Once all of your ingredients are in a pan, measure the depth. Then all you have to do when reducing the liquid, is to keep measuring the depth, until you reach half of the original number.

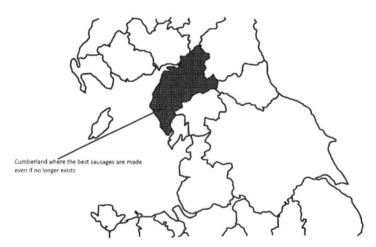

Cumberland where the best sausages are made
even if no longer exists

Component 36
Russian Dressing

This is a great sauce to have on a burger. It's also known as burger sauce or Big Mac sauce (if you add some diced up gherkins and onions).

1tsp	mayo
½tsp	ketchup
½tsp	English mustard
2drops	Tabasco
5drops	Worcestershire sauce

Mix everything together in a bowl.

Component 37
Riata

100g	natural yogurt
1tsp	mint sauce
¼tsp	cumin
½tsp	lemon juice
	salt and pepper

Mix all the ingredients in a bowl and add salt and pepper to taste. Don't be afraid to make it a little mintier than normal, a good hit of mint is great with the koftas.

Component 38
Marie Rose

AKA Thousand Island dressing.

1dsp	tomato ketchup
1dsp	mayo
½tsp	English mustard
4drops	Worcestershire sauce
	salt and pepper

Mix everything together in a bowl.

Component 39
Apple Sauce

Makes around 15 portions.

1. Peel and roughly chop 4 Bramley apples, then sprinkle with lemon juice to stop discolouration.
2. Place in a pan with 2cm depth of water.
3. Simmer gently until the apples fall apart (approx. 15mins).
4. Allow to cool with some lumps left for texture.

Component 40
Therimidor Sauce

½tsp	crushed garlic
10g	butter
100ml	chicken stock
1tsp	Dijon mustard
50ml	white wine
25ml	brandy
¼tsp	parsley (dried)
150ml	double cream
	salt and pepper

1. Sweat the garlic in butter.
2. Add the mustard, stock, white wine, parsley and brandy.
3. Simmer until the liquid has reduced by half.
4. Add the cream and season with salt and pepper to taste.
5. Simmer the cream until thick (be careful not to let the cream burn to the bottom of the pan).
6. Allow to cool. It should be the consistency of clotted cream once cooled.

Component 41
Cheese Sauce

This is a white (or béchamel) sauce with cheese in. There are lots of ways to make a white sauce. I think this is the easiest, even if it isn't the traditional way. Use the way/recipe you are used to using, but for a toastie you want the sauce a little thicker than for most uses of a white sauce.

½ pint	full milk
30g	butter
30g	plain flour
½ tsp	mustard
50g	cheddar (grated)
	salt and pepper

1. Put flour, milk, butter, mustard and salt & pepper in a non-stick sauce pan.
2. Heat slowly while stirring constantly with a silicone whisk.
3. Bring to the boil for 1 min.
4. Take off the heat and add the cheese while stirring.
5. Allow to cool before using in a toastie.

Component 42 Barbeque Sauce

This sauce has a lot of ingredients, but is very easy to make. Once it is made, it is safe to keep in the fridge for a month.

It makes a great marinade or dipping sauce as well.

1tbsp	vegetable oil
1	white onion (diced)
½tsp	cracked black pepper
1tsp	garlic puree
400g	tinned tomatoes
1tsp	English mustard
5tsp	smoked paprika
1½tsp	salt
2dsp	maple syrup
2dsp	maggi liquid seasoning
2dsp	Worcestershire sauce
100ml	malt Vinegar
100g	demerara sugar

1. Sweat the onions and garlic with the pepper.
2. Add all the other ingredients.
3. Simmer for 45 mins.
4. Blitz until smooth ina food processor or with a stick blender.
5. Chill and store in airtight container in the fridge for up to a month.

Component 43
Rarebit Sauce

This recipe uses an ingredient called Henderson's Relish. This is a bit like Worcestershire Sauce but it is vegetarian. However, it is only available in the Sheffield area, so if you don't live in South Yorkshire Worcestershire sauce is a perfectly good replacement.

50g	English mustard
50g	Dijon mustard
3tsp	Henderson's relish
75ml	ale

1. Mix all the ingredients (minus the ale) and stir well.
2. Slowly add the ale while stirring until you have a runny brown sauce consistency.
3. Drink the rest of the beer.

To make Welsh Rarebit, simply make the sauce as above and mix with grated cheddar (it will make a sticky gooey mass of cheese). Put it on some toast and grill. It is also excellent on smoked haddock. Simply make a welsh rarebit mix and put a big handful on a piece of smoked haddock then bake for around 15mins.

Component 44
Marinara Sauce

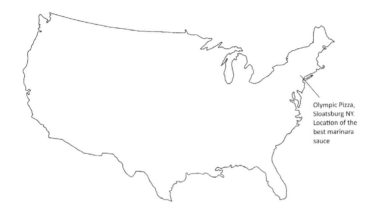

Olympic Pizza,
Sloatsburg NY.
Location of the
best marinara
sauce

The American name for a classic tomato sauce and now that Olympic Pizza has shut down you will have to make your own.

1	onion (finely chopped)
1 stick	celery (finely chopped)
2	garlic cloves
400g	tinned tomatoes
1tbsp	tomato puree
1tsp	mixed herbs
½tsp	lemon juice
½tsp	brown sugar
	salt and pepper
	butter

1. Sweat the onions and celery in butter until soft.
2. Add the garlic and cook for 1 minute.
3. Add the tomatoes and flavouring and simmer gently for 20mins.

B5 Dessert Components

Component 45
Deep Fried Mars Bar

100g   self-raising flour

100g   plain flour

200ml   Black Sheep ale (or any other good quality bitter)

1   standard size Mars bar

Before starting pre-heat a deep fat fryer to 170°C

1. Mix the flour together.
2. Add a little ale at a time and beat well. Once all the lumps are gone add more ale.
3. Keep adding ale until you have a thick batter (about the consistency of syrup).
4. Cut the mars bar into 2 even pieces.
5. Roll each half in plain flour and shake off excess.
6. Spike each half onto a kebab skewer.
7. Dip each into the batter.
8. Hold the mars bar in the middle of the fryer until the batter is set. This stops it sinking and attaching to the basket (they are really hard to get it off again).
9. Fry for around 2 mins or until the batter is golden and fully cooked.
10. DO NOT eat straight away as it will be exactly 1,000,000°C inside.

Component 46
Carnation Caramel

This is also the perfect caramel for Millionaires shortbread. You can buy pre-made carnation caramel, but it isn't quite the right consistency and this is easy to make.

You can make as many cans at the same time as you can fit into the base of a sauce pan. You can also use cheaper supermarket condensed milk, but they tend to have glued-on labels which peal off during the cooking process, then you have to clean the glue and paper off the pan, which is a horrible job and not worth the 26p you save.

1 can   Carnation condensed milk

1. Put the sealed can of condensed milk it into a sauce pan and cover with cold water.
2. Bring the pan to the boil.
3. Turn the heat down to a simmer.
4. Simmer for 3 hours.
5. Allow to cool in the water.
6. If left sealed the caramel will last for weeks.

Do not let the pan boil dry or the can will explode and can cause serious harm. Also, you will be removing toffee from your kitchen for the next 3 years. This is why cans carry a warning.

Component 47
Rocky Road Mix

1tsp	mini marshmallows
1	digestive biscuit (broken into pieces)
½ tsp	dark chocolate buttons
1tsp	milk chocolate buttons
1tsp	white chocolate buttons
1tsp	raisins
1tsp	chocolate spread

Mix until the ingredients have formed a sticky chocolatey ball.

Component 48
Roast Rhubarb

2	stems rhubarb
1tbsp	vegetable oil

1. Chop the rhubarb into 3cm pieces.
2. Toss the rhubarb in oil.
3. Spread onto a baking tray.
4. Roast for 10mins at 180ºC or until soft.

Component 49
Custard

Make Birds Custard in the traditional way, but using the following quantities. This will result in a very sweet custard that has the consistency of melted cheese...perfect for a toastie.

½pint milk
½pint single cream
100g sugar
60g custard powder
3drops vanilla essence

1. Mix the sugar and custard powder with a little of the milk to form a paste.
2. Heat the milk and cream until nearly boiling.
3. Pour the milk/cream over the custard mix while stirring constantly.
4. Return the mix to the pan and heat gently while stirring until it has thickened.

The back of bird packets have now changed and recommend a different method. I use the old way so these quantities are all based the old fashioned technique.

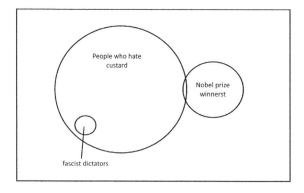

Component 50 Mincemeat

This recipe has come through at least 5 Generations of my Mum's family (Mary, Gwen, Jane, Liz, Barny). Each person has tweaked it a little. This my version, but is essentially the same as it was 150 years ago (although it was probably in imperial back then). If you are making this you do need a meat mincer: use the medium blade.

500g	raisins
500g	currants
500g	sultanas
500g	dried figs
200g	glacé cherries
7	large bramley apples, peeled, cored and roughly chopped
100g	dried apricots
250g	pitted dates
400g	suet
750g	soft brown sugar
1	lemon (zest & Juice)
1	orange (zest & Juice)
½tsp	nutmeg
½tsp	mixed spice
½tsp	cinnamon
½tsp	ginger
½tsp	mace

1. Mince together half of the raisins, currents, sultanas and all of the cherries, dates, figs, apricots and apples.
2. Mix in the rest of the fruit, sugar, suet and spices.
3. Store in an airtight container in a cool dark place for up to a month.

Component 51
Brandy Butter

250g   butter (salted)

75ml   brandy

250g   soft brown sugar

Put everything into a mixer and beat until it has gone very pale, fluffy and the butter feels less grainy.

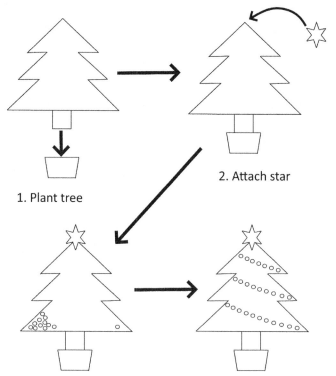

1. Plant tree

2. Attach star

3. Children hang up ornaments

4. Redistribute ornaments

Section C: Other Information

Butter goes on the outside

To make a toastie the first thing you need to know is that butter goes on the outside of the sandwich. For most this is common knowledge, for the rest it will sound weird, be counter-intuitive and feel unnatural when you are first making a toasted sandwich.

As the toastie cooks, the butter allows the bread to form a beautiful crispy layer, and turn the delicious golden brown you are looking for. You can avoid butter, but when you cook your creation the bread will dry out rather than crisping up. Throughout the book the recipes call for buttered bread, this always needs to have the butter on the outside for cooking.

Storage

If you need to make some toasties for cooking later. This is a great way to feed people without having to spend all the time you are entertaining in the kitchen. If you make them, stack them and put them in the fridge, strange and unexpected things can happen. The butter on the outside of your toasties will go hard in the cold which means that they need to be separated. The best thing for this is grease-proof paper between each layer. Believe me when I say that we have found out the hard way that without these grease-proof layers the toastie stack will become a useless behemoth of bread, cheese and meat.

If you are storing, it is also advisable to use spreadable butter rather than just normal butter so that it's easier to get them apart.

If you are freezing toasties, only freeze sanwiches that are made of mainly dry ingredients. Ham and cheese will freeze and deforst perfectly, others like the tuna melt will not!

Grated or Sliced Cheese?

In the toasted sandwich community there is a fierce debate on sliced or grated cheese. We have found that slices are better for 5 reasons:

1. Sliced cheese stays fresher. It has a smaller surface area to volume ratio so the speed at which the taste degrades is slower than that of grated.
2. When dealing with 80kg of cheese, slicing is a lot easier than grating and once prepared takes up a lot less room. Although, I expect this is less of an issue for most people.
3. When making toasties, grated cheese is very messy and therefore wasteful
4. You can get more cheese into a toasties if it is sliced as apposed to grated. Grated cheese looks impressive before it is melted, but what you need to worry about is what the final product tastes like.
5. Sliced cheese will melt more slowly than grated. This gives the outside of your toastie more time to cook and therefore it will be crispier once finished which is a good thing.

The slower melt from sliced cheese does mean that some of the thicker toasties are hard to melt and difficult to fit into a traditional toastie machine. However, the advantages of sliced outweigh this problem; just cook them for a bit longer and everything will be fine.

A final point on grated cheese, if you decide to ignore the above and use grated anyway, please use freshly grated not pre-grated. The pre-grated cheese has a coating on (usually potato starch) to stop it clumping. This does not melt well and will impair the cheese delight that should be your toastie.

Important Cheese Information

Cheddar is the cheese we use the most and it is worth finding a really good one. We have found that a mature cheddar is about right. A medium will be a little too weak whilst with extra mature the meltabilty will not be as good. Hunt around for a locally made "cheddar". It might cost more and be a bit harder to find but it will be better than the insipid taste of Cathedral City that we are all so used to.

The cheese we use is made by the oldest cheese maker in England (Fowler's of Earlswood). Who are based just 20 miles up the road. When eaten "raw" I am not a big fan. However, once melted this really is an amazing cheese. It is smooth, rich and tastes completely different. The moral of this story is try it cold, but also try a cheese melted you might be pleasantly surprised.

It is worth pointing out that some cheeses should not be used in a toastie. Stilton does not melt properly. It will split when heated and the resultant mess is very strong tasting and over powers everything else. We have overcome this problem (see component 20), but beware. Other problem melters are very mature cheeses (cheddar etc.). As a cheese ages, it gets a stronger taste but also becomes harder to melt. Eventually the same thing happens as with stilton, and instead of melting it splits into curds and grease. Crumbly cheeses (like Wensleydale, Cheshire and Lancashire) will not melt whatever you do to them, so if you want to use them they need to be treated like the stilton as described.

Finally: quality over quantity. You will get a much nicer toastie with a smaller amount of expensive cheese than one made with lots of cheap cheese.

Bread

I recommend white bread for pretty much every toastie (notable exceptions are numbers 11 and 29). This is because it has the most neutral flavour, so you can enjoy the filling more. Plus is will go crispy much better than brown or rye. However, some of our toasties are fantastic on brown, so have a play and remember there is no perfect toastie (although I am always searching for it).

If you prefer a particular type of bread go with that. Remember; just because a bread makes a great sandwich, it does not mean that it makes great toast. Experiment and test; it is the best and tastiest approach to toasties.

The best thickness for the bread is medium. Thick sliced bread might look like you are being generous, but this means you need more filling to keep the bread:filling ratio correct. By using thick bread we have found you need to more than double the amount of fillings to compensate for the extra dough. It takes much much longer to melt the fillings and makes getting properly crispy toast very difficult.

How long do you cook a toastie?

As a guide usually a round 3minutes, but there is no hard and fast rule regarding this. A lot depends on the toastie press you are using and how high you have it set (usually at max). But the time also depends on the type of cheese inside and the thickness of the ingredients used particularly the bread.

When cooking you need to balance the need to have melted cheese with not burning the outside. Golden brown is the colour you want!

Types of Toastie Press

There are 2 main types of toastie press out there (ignoring making it in a pan with a weight). There is the traditional toastie maker (like the Breville from your childhood). This will create 2 rounds of sandwich, with the edges sealed and the characteristic triangle shaped pockets on the bread. Then there is the panini style grill, with flat plates. Both types have their advantages. We tend to use a panini style grill, as it means we can cook more and you can fit more stuff inside them. It also allows you to make double and triple decker toasties. However, they don't look like a traditional toastie and they are liable to leak during the cooking process. No one wants to lose precious melted cheese.

Whatever machine you decide to make a toastie on, make sure that you clean it after use and don't use metal utensils as these destroy the non-stick coating on the plates. The instructions should tell you how to season the plates before use.

Make sure that your chosen press is switched on and hot before your toasties are loaded in. When the toastie hits the press there should be an audible sizzle and that tells you this is going to be golden brown and delicious in 3 minutes time.

To Butter or Not To Butter?

If you ask the internet there is some disagreement about what should be put on the outside of a toasted sandwich (as mentioned previously the butter goes on the outside). The choice come down to 3 options, butter, oil or mayo. I have ignored margarine as, it doesn't taste good, is not healthy, cooks poorly and is no easier to use than the others.

Oil

Oil is difficult to spread around, but is the healthy option. Unfortunately if you leave the sandwiches in the fridge for any length of time the oil can sink into the bread and lead to greasy soggy mess rather than toasties.

It is an excellent option for vegan or dairy free toasties, but must be used sparingly.

Mayonnaise

Mayo is easy to use, and ready to go. I know what you are thinking; "it'll taste weird". It really doesn't. Mayo is almost entirely oil with a bit of vinegar. Once cooked it has almost no taste which makes it a good option for the outside of your toasties.

Butter

My choice is butter or spreadable butter. Butter will make your toasted sandwich taste like the toasties you remember from childhood or like the ones we serve. It has the best flavour and will give you a lovely deep, rich, golden colour when cooked.

The main problem with butter is that it's hard to spread on bread. For ease and taste we use our own homemade spreadable butter, but this is only really worth doing if you are making dozens of toasties. If you are just making 1 or 2, microwave a small amount of butter and use that or buy some spreadable butter. We have found the lurpak spreadable to be the best of the ready to go options.

How to De-glaze

This is a process by which you get every grain of flavour into your food. It's a very useful trick to learn and can improve the taste of many dishes. It's best done with wine as it contains alcohol which is a universal solvent.

Deglazing has one other great advantage it will do a lot of the cleaning of the roasting dish (or frying pan) for you.

1. Once you have removed a meat item from a pan/roasting dish: pour away any fat.
2. Put a glass of wine into the pan.
3. Heat the pan on the stove.
4. As the wine heats use a spatula to clean the brown residue from the pan (the glaze).
5. Boil the wine to remove most of the alcohol.
6. Add the wine (which now contains a whole lot of extra flavour) into the meat or sauce you are about to eat.

Troubleshooting

Problem	Error Code	Probable Cause	Solution
Toastie falls apart after or during cooking	AFATTIESOIL	Not enough cheese	More cheese
		Cheese not on both sides of the other ingredients	Spread cheese more evenly through the sandwich
		Press not squashing the toastie together enough	Add weight to the toastie press
Bland Toastie	BANALDITTOES	Poor Quality ingredients	Buy better quality Ingredients
		Lack of seasoning	Add a little salt
		Not enough cheese	More cheese
Anaemic exterior, boiling hot filling	PEATOTALS	Toastie press is not hot enough	Turn the toatie press to a higher temperature
			Make sure the press is hot before you put your sandwich on it (listen for a sizzle)
Dark brown toast and un-melted cheese	ELMIGININOT	Toastie press is too hot	Turn the press down to a lower temperature

Barny Luxmoore

Acknowledgements and Thanks

Thanks to Flic for being with me on our journey in street food and the extra child wrangling so I could get this book finished. Also for proof reading and not making too much fun of me after finding many ridiculous mistakes.

The COVID-19 lockdown for motivating me to get this finished (I started the book 5 years ago). All other aspects of COVID-19 have sucked.

Mum and Dad for proof reading this book.

Laurence, Emma, Emma, Dom, Jack, Sarah, Becky and Victoria for your hard work with us over the years at many many events. Also all our friends who helped out when we couldn't afford to pay staff: Monty, Amy, Spanky, Rachel, Beth, Corinne, James, Dom, Eilidh, Will.

Monty for being my date to award ceremonies and for your excellent design work through the years.

All our regular and irregular customers whom we have got to know over the last decade and who have made it possible for us to have a job that is so much fun. Sorry if I don't know your name (or I have forgotten it): John & Gemma, Rowan, Sam, Tom & partner, Claire (the rest of the Leamington gamers), Sean, Sarah & John, Ben, Pieter, Mike, Robin, Harry, Charlotte, Chloe & Dave, Charles, Jamie, Scott, Jenny, Ollie, Alison, Steph & Chappie, Dawn, Vindi, Sexy Ian, Dan, Amy, Emma & Toby, Lucy, Cal & Anya, Chris, Paul, Hannah, Nuno, Lynn, Chris, Andy, Paul, Neil, Paul and Rachel, AShleigh, Steve, Cats-protection-guy, Couple who live on Leamington Parade, Tall Manwich eating ginger beard (not customers Becky & Frank, Eva & Craig).

West's, Highams, Fowler's and Galileo Farm thank you for your excellent food over the years.

Name That Quote

When we are out and about we always have a movie quote on a blackboard for people to try and guess. Correct answers win some sweets. It seemed wrong not to include some, here are 10 movie quotes to try and figure out. Sorry no prizes this time. Answers are on page 139.

Life moves pretty fast. If you don't stop and look around once in a while, you could miss it.

We're all pretty bizarre, some of us are just better at hiding it.

You've got red on you.

No your other left.

Hope is a good thing, maybe even the best of things and no good thing ever dies.

Somebody get this walking carpet out of my way!

If my calculations are correct, when this baby hits 88 miles per hour, you're gonna see some serious shit.

We came, we saw, we kicked its ass!

You know, for kids.

Is it better to be feared or respected?

Contact Details

If you want to get in touch then below are all the ways I am avaliable. Most of these are contacts for The Jabberwocky as I don't really do personal social media, so you might get Flic answering you (you will definately get Flic on facebook).

www.thejabberwocky.co.uk

Facebook @jabberwockyfood

Instagram @jabberwockyfood

Twitter @jabberwockyfood

email barnyluxmoore@gmail.com

Name That Quote Answers

For those that care, here are the answer to "name that quote".

Ferris Bueller's Day Off

The Breakfast Club

Shaun of the Dead

The Matrix

The Shawshank Redemption

Star Wars: A New Hope

Back to the Future

Ghostbusters

The Hudsucker Proxy

Ironman